UN-CONVENT[...]

13 YEARS OF MEETIN[...]

KAREN LC[...]

To Jake—
Love from,
[signature]

Un-conventional
Karen Louise Hayward

First Published in the UK in September 2010 by 100 Publishing
An imprint of Hirst Publishing

Hirst Publishing, Suite 285 Andover House, George Yard, Andover,
Hants, SP10 1PB

ISBN 978-1-907959-07-3

Cover Design by Robert Hammond

Printed and bound by Good News Digital Books

Paper stock used is natural, recyclable and made from wood grown in
sustainable forests. The manufacturing processes conform to
environmental regulations.

www.hirstbooks.com

ACKNOWLEDGEMENTS

To my Dad – for getting me into Doctor Who in the first place and reading me endless Target novelisations.

To Nik – for proof-reading, formatting and reading this book many times without complaining (too much!). Also for being there for these 13 years and coping with my endless droning on about gorgeous celebs!

To Colin Baker – (Talking about gorgeous celebs…) Thanks for the inspiration, the friendship and all the cuddles and autographs.

To my kids – Leigh-Ann, Dom, Emilia and Viki. I hope you enjoy seeing your name in the book and that your years as Doctor Who fans continue!

To my lovely family – Mum, Lynn and Beth, Glynis and Terry, Gran and everyone. Thanks for everything!

To Robert Shearman – for your time and interest and inspiration.

To the friends I've made over the years at conventions especially Trevor Fennell, Ben Melberg, Tristan Maddocks and Jason Thomas. Love you guys!

Thanks to any online reference sources I've used, especially IMDB and Wikipedia.

Thanks to Tim Hirst for believing in the book.

Remembering
John Nathan-Turner
and
Anthony Ainley

1997 was a momentous year.

On January 23rd, I met Colin Baker for the first time.

On July 25th, I met my future husband.

Twenty years earlier, when I was a child watching Tom Baker's Doctor with my Dad on Saturday evenings, I never could have guessed how important Doctor Who would become in my life…

Chapter One
The Early Years

Being born in 1969, my Doctor was Tom Baker. Saturday television was the highlight of the week for me. Dad would finish work at the Lincolnshire Echo newspaper and we would sit down to an evening of family entertainment. At various times, this included Basil Brush (boom boom!), The Generation Game, Jim'll Fix It, the football results and – of course! - Doctor Who.

One of the stories that most sticks in my mind from this time is Planet of the Spiders. As I would have only been four when it was on, I am inclined to believe my memories come more from the Target novelisation with its terrifying picture on the front. That giant spider on Sarah Jane's back haunted me for years and is possibly responsible for the arachnophobia I suffered with for decades.

We had a lot of the Target books, so Dad read me those at bedtime and I later read them myself. I know I tended to picture Tom Baker as the Doctor in all the stories, even if he hadn't been the actor in the role at the time. The ones I recall from childhood are those published in 1975 and 1976. The Daemons was another one with a scary cover, which I had to turn over if it was on my bedside table! One of my favourites was The Three Doctors, which had Hartnell, Troughton and Pertwee on the cover, Omega's big hands on top of their heads in a menacing fashion.

I was aware of the other actors who had played the Doctor though. I found an old exercise book of mine from about 1976 and inside it are lists and stories I've written, which include references to various Doctor Who characters and cast members – Benton, Omega, Tom Baker, Jon Pertwee ("Pertwea"), William Hartnell, Patrick Troughton

("Thoughton"), Sarah Jane Smith, Harry, Bok, Dinosaurs, Daleks ("Darleks"), Bellal, Davros, Ogrons ("Ograns"), Exxilons, Spiders, the Queen Spider, Daemons ("Deamons"), Cybermen, Ice Warriors, Yetis, Sea Devils, Jo Grant and Zygons!

I met Tom Baker in Lincoln, when he came to do a book signing in Woolworth's. (Picture next page courtesy of the Lincolnshire Echo.) Mum took me along into town and we queued through the shop. I think it must have been 1976, as that was the publication year of my edition of the Genesis of the Daleks book he signed. I still have it; the autograph says "To Karen, Doctor Who?"

Besides Tom, the other Doctor Who star I met as a child was Frazer Hines. We saw him in panto at the Theatre Royal, Lincoln in December 1982, when he was co-starring with Tracie Bennett and I met them both afterwards. My parents took me to the theatre a lot and Mum always encouraged me to meet the stars and get their autographs. It's a habit I still continue.

I got a Doctor Who doll for Christmas 1978, the one based on Tom Baker. When I later got a Princess Leia doll from Star Wars, I decided she looked like Mary Tamm's Romana, so called her Princess Leia Romana. I rarely paired them up though, my Tom Baker doll had a crush on my Ballerina Sindy!

I loved Tom Baker. He reminded me of my Dad as they both had big curly hair and were always smiling. The Doctor was a real hero and you could always trust him to get out of danger and save the world.

While Tom was my Doctor, my favourite companion was definitely Sarah Jane Smith. I thought she was great and really admired her. I remember being upset when she left the series on my 7th birthday – October 23rd 1976. How rude!

My favourite enemy were the Cybermen. Therefore, you would expect the combination of my favourite Doctor, my favourite companion and my favourite enemy all together would produce a perfect story. No, we got Revenge of the Cybermen! Oh dear. One image I do vividly recall from childhood was the hand moving by itself in The Hand of Fear. That was a much better story.

While the Tom Baker era was essential viewing in our household, Peter Davison's tenure was less impressive. I know I watched it at least occasionally, but my diaries from the time hardly mention it, although Adric's demise in Earthshock impressed my 12-year-old self enough to comment that the episode was "ace".

In 1985, I reported about the hiatus in my diary too. Then aged fifteen, I noted "Doctor Who is going to be off T.V. for eighteen months as the BBC want to do new drama things."

I grew up and in 1988, I moved to Portsmouth to go to University. I ended up quitting Uni, but stayed in the city for eight years, getting married and having four children. It was in the 1990s that I rediscovered my passion for Doctor Who, as a friend of mine had Sky and would tape episodes of Doctor Who off UK Gold for me.

I also started re-reading my Target novelisations which I had kept from childhood. A second-hand bookshop near me then began selling someone's collection, so I bought some from there and my own collection increased.

I moved back to Lincolnshire in 1996. That Christmas, the Theatre Royal in Lincoln featured Dick Whittington as its pantomime, starring Colin Baker as King Rat. Being a mother of young children, going to see a panto seemed a very natural thing to do…

Chapter Two
When It All Began (Again)…

The first time I went to see Dick Whittington in Lincoln was on December 27th, 1996. My Dad was already going, as he had to review it for work. He was the Leisure and Entertainments Editor of the Lincolnshire Echo newspaper and also wrote for The Stage. As I had recently got back into Doctor Who again, I asked if I could go along too, just to see Colin Baker and hopefully meet him.

The panto itself was very impressive and a much higher standard than I had remembered them being. There was a Doctor Who theme to it with Colin stepping out of a TARDIS early on, I recall. The highlight for me was the rock 'n' roll number Colin did as King Rat. It was a kind of mix between The Rocky Horror Show and Elvis - and Colin wore tights for it!

I was smitten. He was two years older than my Dad (exactly two years, as I found out later, both June 8th!) but still very attractive. I really wanted to meet him. We waited in the Theatre Royal bar, the usual meeting place for the actors to come and socialise. I had met many great stars in that bar over the years, since I began going to the theatre in the 1970s. Would I be able to add Colin to the list?

No, not that night. The rest of the cast came up, but no Colin. We spoke to Art Walker, who worked at the theatre and he said Colin usually went to the bar and was happy to sign autographs and pose for photos. I vowed to go to the panto another night and try again!

1997 arrived and on January 8th, I went to the panto again, this time with my Mum, my Grandma and my middle daughter Emilia, who was almost four years old. She found

12

Colin's King Rat very scary and wanted to go home in the first half, but we persevered and she enjoyed it by the end.

We stayed afterwards to meet the cast, who made a fuss of little Emilia. She especially liked Lisa Love (who was the fairy), Rhianydd-Lesley Jones (Dick), Christine Walton (Alice) and Bobby Dazzler who played one of the comedy sidekicks. But no sign of Colin again.

I gave Lisa one of the drawings I had done of Colin and she said she would put it on his desk in the dressing room.

Eleven days later, I was back! This time, my Dad had come to see the show again but we also brought my Nanna (who had just turned 90) and my eldest daughter Leigh-Ann who was six years old – proof indeed that pantomime is for every age! Again, it was very good and by this stage, I knew it well enough to spot any additions or errors, which added an extra dimension to my viewing pleasure.

When the panto had finished, we found the bar was shut, so Dad wanted to leave straight away, but I decided to wait outside the Green Room door with Leigh-Ann. One of the dancers came out and he popped in to the dressing room to see if Colin was there, but he had already left. The dancer suggested I come back during the week and try to catch him then.

We saw Bobby Dazzler again and he said both he and Colin were going to the Australian breakfast, which is held at the Lawn in Lincoln every year during panto season. I thought that might be another opportunity to meet my idol.

My fourth visit to see Dick Whittington was four days later on January 23rd and I finally got my wish! This time, my friend Lesley came with me (I was running out of kids and grandparents!) and the bar was closed once more, so we waited outside the Green Room and out he came!

He was very friendly and we all chatted for quite a while.

He said he had got the letter I had sent him and the drawing. He said he had liked the review my Dad had written for The Stage and joked that I should go to all his performances, to get them to write good reviews.

He signed a video sleeve and my Doctor Who magazine, I took a photo of him, then Lesley took one of us together, so I got a cuddle! You can see a photo of us together on the opposite page. Colin was wearing his red jacket which he seemed to wear a lot during the late 1990s, as I discovered in future meetings!

We talked about our big families (four kids each) and our pets. He commented that he was pleased to have our support in the audience, as that night the crowd had been cheering a lot for Cy Chadwick who was one of the leading names in the panto, as he was playing a main character in Emmerdale (Nick Bates) at the time.

We chatted about the ad-libs and the risqué bits the cast added in sometimes. He said Christine Walton (Alice) had flashed her bottom at him from the wings, so when he had picked her up on stage, he had done it at an angle so the audience could see her knickers!

He apologised about not being able to meet me earlier, but explained he had been suffering with a chest infection so hadn't felt up to drinking in the bar. He had received messages from other cast members that I had been trying to meet him though.

I got a kiss too and he said "I can't remember the last time I kissed a 27-year-old!" so Lesley asked about a 37-year-old and got one too! I told him where we would be sitting for the last performance and he said he'd try to throw me a jelly rat, quipping that it was nice to have groupies who were older than twelve!

The Australian Breakfast and the last show of Dick Whittington were both that Sunday, January 26th. I went to the Breakfast with Lesley, her husband and son and two of my daughters.

Most of the cast were in attendance – Colin, Barry Cheese, Bobby Dazzler, Lisa Love, Rhianydd-Lesley Jones, Christine Walton and Cy Chadwick. I didn't find Cy very easy to talk to. I said he looked tired and he took it in the wrong way, saying he had been doing the show for weeks. Bobby was lovely and very nice again. Colin was a bit quiet, but still friendly and I took a couple of photos of him with my daughters.

The show was that evening and I went to the Stage Door with Lesley beforehand. Bobby came out and I gave him some flowers, plus a bouquet of yellow roses to pass on to Colin.

The performance was great fun as there were all sorts of jokes and pranks, with it being the final show. When Bobby said the gag about a boxer dog, I threw a cuddly one onto the stage which Bobby picked up and used as a prop during the scene.

When Colin entered with his jelly rats, I put up a "We

15

love you, King Rat" banner and Colin threw me a rat, as he had promised to. Later on, I put a cuddly (Roland) rat on the edge of the stage for him.

Afterwards, Lesley and I waited outside the Green Room and Colin came out, gave me a kiss and a hug and thanked me for the card and the rat. Bobby came out then and said Lesley and I could go to the bar with him, as there was a farewell party for the cast. As they lived locally, Frazer Hines and Liz Hobbs were at the party too and they spent some time talking to Colin.

The pantomime was over. I had been to five performances of Dick Whittington and enjoyed every one. Colin Baker was my new obsession!

Since I had fallen back in love with Doctor Who, I had been watching the stories on video, buying Doctor Who Magazine each month and I had started writing to the stars to get their autographs. The first reply came back in February. I had written to Louise Jameson at the National Theatre where she had been doing Death of a Salesman and she sent me a letter and signed photo.

The latest issue of Doctor Who Magazine featured an advert for something called Travellers in Time based in Llangollen, North Wales. I rang them for details and found that Colin Baker was going to be the special guest for the March weekend! It sounded wonderful. It was limited to just forty people, meals and accommodation were included, as well as train and boat trips, a trip round the Doctor Who exhibition, evening entertainment and it was all hosted by John Nathan-Turner!

The only problem was that it cost £169 plus transport costs and spending money. I could afford the £40 deposit from my wages as a part-time barmaid, but the rest would be hard to find. I sorted out some of my Madonna and Marilyn Monroe collections to sell and went up in my parents' loft to look for anything else I could use to raise the money. I was determined to go. I really wanted to see Colin again.

A few days later, I received a letter and some fan club magazines from Colin. They arrived on the day my Mum walked out on my Dad, so gave me some comfort during a miserable time.

I had recently finished reading Doctor Who: The Handbook – The Third Doctor by David J. Howe and Stephen James Walker. I looked round Lincoln for the Sixth Doctor one, but could only find the books on Jon, Tom and Peter's years in the role. I ordered the Sixth Doctor Handbook from W H Smith's and it arrived a couple of weeks later. I could now find out more about the Sixth Doctor, as I had hardly watched it during those years, when I had been a moody teenager!

I had written a letter to Chris Moreno, the Director of the Theatre Royal, Lincoln to say how much I had enjoyed seeing Colin there and hoped he would return again in the near future. I got a reply from Chris saying he hoped Colin would be back soon too.

I persuaded my Dad to go on the Llangollen weekend with me and he paid for some of the holiday too, as we both needed the break. As well as going through his own relationship problems, I was also in an unhappy marriage and felt a few days away would be beneficial for everyone.

The weekend was March 14th to 16th. The guests were Colin and Wendy Padbury, as well as John Nathan-Turner (JNT) and his partner, Gary Downie, who were both part of the team behind the Travellers in Time weekends. The whole concept was such a great idea - small gatherings where you enjoyed a weekend away in a hotel in the most beautiful part of the country, sharing almost every waking moment with the celebrities. Idyllic.

It was also a great opportunity to meet new friends and

find others who shared your passion for the programme and its stars. Dad and I met two guys from South Wales – Trevor Fennell and Ben Melberg – at this weekend and got on brilliantly with them. We went round with them for this weekend and have met up several times over the years.

The weekend's events began at 2pm on the Friday and included a Trivia Quiz hosted by JNT at 4pm. When Colin walked in to the room, he pointed at me and said "I know you! You've had your hair cut!" to which I said "So have you!" I was pleased he had recognised me.

I had written a Doctor Who themed story about him, based around the pantomime called 'Doctor Who – Link-On' and had laboriously typed out several thousand words of it (on an old typewriter), giving him a copy. He read it that night and after noting the many flattering bits in it, he suggested I should have my glasses changed!

Gary Downie talked about his jobs on Doctor Who (Assistant Floor Manager, Location Manager and Choreographer) from 5:30 to 6:30pm. He was very outspoken and candid and was not the kind of person you wanted to get on the wrong side of, as he could be incredibly bitchy and even vitriolic about people he disliked. He hated Anthony Ainley and never seemed to tire of poking fun at him and criticising him!

He had brought some photographs to show us that came from the shoot for The Two Doctors, when the cast and crew had gone to Seville for filming. The atmosphere had been a good one in Spain, almost like a holiday with everyone in the same place together and I seem to recall Gary's photos including several of Nicola Bryant in the swimming pool. He was quite scathing about her at times, complaining that she always seemed to be feeling ill.

Gary's talk was followed by an hour-long chat from Colin Baker. One of my favourite stories was about his daughter Lucy who went to school with Peter Davison's daughter Georgia Moffett. At school one day when they were young, the teacher was asking what each child's parents did as an occupation. Georgia piped up "My Dad's Doctor Who!" "So's mine!" retorted Lucy.

Lucy was doing a production of Jonah at school and Colin said he needed to buy a camcorder for it. He said his daughters were into the Spice Girls (like mine were). He had passed A-levels in French, Latin and Greek and said he hadn't been able to drink alcohol for a while as he had been ill with the chest infection in Lincoln and was now on antibiotics for his teeth.

It was dinner in the hotel restaurant at 8:30pm. Colin had recently written an article for the Bucks Free Press about how 'nit-nurses' had been dropped from schools now, so we had a good chat about head lice. That whetted our appetite for dinner!

Wendy Padbury's talk was from 10pm to 11pm, followed by charades. The game was lots of fun and all the stars joined in enthusiastically, so we ended up staying up until 2am playing it!

Colin suggested we played a prank on John Nathan-Turner by pretending not to be able to guess his mime, no matter what he did. It was really funny! JNT was getting more and more frustrated, trying different ways to mime it and puzzled by our apparent ignorance. It took a while before he cottoned on to what was happening, but he saw the joke once he twigged. He was a really good sport and we had a lot of laughs with him.

The Saturday began with a group trip to the nearby Doctor Who Experience and its adjoining model railway museum and Canal Boat museum. All the celebs were involved with this and there were plenty of photo opportunities too. This included having a ride with Colin and Wendy in Bessie 2, a replica of the original prop, which itself was a part of the exhibition.

The afternoon trip was a narrow boat trip along the

terrifying Pontcysyllte Aqueduct - 126 feet above the River Dee! Being phobic about heights, I spent a lot of this trip hiding down close to the floor of the boat, determined to NOT look over the edge.

At one point, Colin and I were singing the Rosie and Jim theme tune and chatting about children's TV. As our children were similar ages, we could sympathise about enduring endless repeats of our kids' favourite programmes. I told Colin that John Cunliffe who presented Rosie and Jim was also the writer of the Postman Pat stories. Colin said he would often read to his children at bedtime, but had been known to fall asleep himself in the process!

Continuing along the Llangollen canal, Colin told us all of a previous weekend he had been at. They had organised another boat trip along the Aqueduct and as they were coming up to the restaurant, a Cybermen invasion had been planned! They had several men dressed in the Cybermen costumes, hiding ready for the boat to appear. As it came along the canal, the Cybermen jumped aboard it ready to surprise the Doctor Who fans. However – they had got the wrong boat! Instead of the fans they expected, it was just a boat full of ordinary holidaymakers and they had to make a swift retreat. Whoops!

We all got out at the Wharf restaurant for a Question and Answer session with Colin, Wendy, John and Gary. This was when Wendy talked about idolising the prima ballerina Svetlana Beriosova. As she said this, Gary piped up with "Oooh, I met her!" and then Wendy was full of questions wanting to know how, why and where!

After our evening meal back in the hotel, it was karaoke from 10pm onwards. The man running it got all his gear together and enthusiastically announced it, but the expected rush of volunteers never materialised (Ha!) and the awkward silence continued. So – for some unknown reason, in a moment of rashness – I offered to sing a solo – but only if Colin would reward me with a kiss. He agreed and I launched into an extremely wobbly rendition of The Bangles classic Eternal Flame, which deserves to be forgotten forever. After I finished, I walked off and Colin was standing there to meet me and gave me a big kiss. Sigh. It was worth all the nerves for that.

The Sunday saw us return to the Doctor Who exhibition and have a tour of the Dapol factory, where the Doctor Who model figures were made. During the factory tour, I gave Colin my diary to write an inscription in, which he did. It was at this point that I proposed to him! I can't remember exactly what I said and I admit I said it in a jokey way, but his response was "I'm married" and mine was "So am I!" If he had been single though (and interested!), I certainly know I could have left my unhappy marriage fairly easily.

But events continued and all of us met up at Llangollen Station around noon on the Sunday for a trip on the steam railway together and our lunch. This was the final part of our wonderful weekend and after bidding fond farewells, it was back home to Lincolnshire and back to normality.

Colin Baker with me in Llangollen 1997

It wasn't too long before all things Who popped into my

life though. Nicola Bryant was coming to the Theatre Royal, Lincoln in April, so I rang Doctor Who Magazine to see if they would be interested in me interviewing her for them, but they said no, as they had recently done one with her.

I went to see the play anyway, of course, along with my friend Lesley. It was Home Truths by Rosemary Friedman and was set in Norfolk over a Christmas weekend. It was well-acted, but rather deep and depressing. The cast included Christopher Cazenove, Edward Hardwicke, Estelle Skornik (Nicole in the Renault adverts) and Lynda Baron, but it was Nicola I had come to see.

I met her afterwards and she was very sweet and friendly, as well as being beautiful. She said she didn't like signing the colour bikini picture of her in the Doctor Who: Companions book (by David J. Howe and Mark Stammers), but was happy to autograph the black and white one of her on the next page – which she did. She also signed the Doctor Who postcard I had of her and Lesley took a photo of us together.

Colin Baker was on television quite a lot in 1997. In April, he featured as Donald Dewhurst in four episodes of The Knock, a drama series set in a Customs and Excise office. I didn't usually watch it, but made a special effort so as to see Colin in his latest TV role. He was in an episode of Jonathan Creek on May 10th, played a judge in Hollyoaks in June and was in The Bill in November, so I watched those too.

On May 4th, I went to my first ever Doctor Who convention – Manopticon in Manchester. I persuaded Dad to come with me, so he drove us there.

The guests featured two Doctors - Tom Baker and Sylvester McCoy, eight companions – Sarah Sutton, Matthew Waterhouse, Mark Strickson, Sophie Aldred, Caroline John, Elisabeth Sladen, Wendy Padbury and Michael Craze, and three of the UNIT team – Nicholas Courtney, John Levene and Richard Franklin, along with Terry Molloy, Terrance Dicks, William Gaunt and Mark Eden.

It was a tiring day and the hotel was very hot with the hall completely packed most of the time. There were apparently over 800 fans there and as there were cut-off points for the autograph queues, I only managed to meet two of the actors, though they were the two I most wanted – Tom Baker (who signed for three hours and promised to give autographs to everyone who wanted one) and Sylvester McCoy.

Both were very friendly and I had my photo taken with them. I told Sylvester I had written to him and he said "It'll be replied to, I'm sure." (It wasn't.) He asked where I was from and I said Lincoln, but it was quite hard to hear. The autograph sessions were in an upstairs room looking out over the main hall. This meant the attendees could follow the stage panels while they were queuing, but consequently the noise level was higher than usual.

When I met Tom Baker, I told him I had met him some twenty years earlier (at the Woolworth's signing of the Target books) so he wrote 'To Karen, 20 years on! Tom Baker.'

He was the most impressive and entertaining speaker too and received a very long and warm standing ovation when he walked onto the stage. When it finally went quiet and the applause died down, he announced "There's a perfect example of the power of fiction!"

He went straight into one of his wonderful anecdotes.
He'd been in Chicago in a temperature of 140F (60C – believe it if you wish, ha!) with a queue of 1500 fans, who were mostly women. In a reckless moment ("because there's a touch of St Francis of Assisi in me") and because the first lady looked "so desperate" and had been waiting for hours, he embraced her. Then the word went along the line - "You get embraced!" so he had to embrace the other 1499 sweating women! He reassured the audience - "I've got nothing against sweaty women. I've had some very pleasant encounters with sweaty women!"

His talk included such revelations as his like for Charles Dickens, his ownership of Burmese cats and that he was planning to have his autobiography published by the autumn. (Who On Earth Is Tom Baker? was indeed published later in 1997.)

I saw some of the other panels, including the Wendy Padbury and Michael Craze one. Wendy commented that out of the monsters she worked with, she found the Ice Warriors the most frightening. However she liked the Cybermen very much and thought they looked great, but they hadn't scared her.

Elisabeth Sladen and Caroline John were interviewed together. Lis was asked if she had been given her own K9 to keep. She replied she had never even been given a K9 and Company video, never mind a proper model!

I sat in the fifth row for the Mark Strickson interview, so

took some photos of him. He was very good-looking! He walked onto the stage holding a pint and wearing a smart beige waistcoat. He showed some clips of the films he had been producing about crocodiles and snakes. He talked about life in Australia, loving British beer and being passionate about conservation. He said he was a vegetarian and into green issues, warning that overcrowding and consumerism were the two most important things threatening the planet.

The UNIT panel consisted of Nicholas Courtney, Richard Franklin and John Levene being interviewed together. John could be quite loud and dramatic and dominated proceedings somewhat. Nick got a big round of applause when he announced his book would be out soon. (Five Rounds Rapid was released in 1998.)

Matthew Waterhouse came over very well and was eloquent and intelligent. He was on stage with Sarah Sutton. They were asked about how they would compare working with Tom Baker to working with Peter Davison. Matthew "always adored" Tom and adored his work, saying Tom was sweet, funny and made you laugh, but could also be frightening and intimidating. Peter was very different - sweet, incredibly together and amazingly easy to work with.

Sarah agreed Tom was harder to work with, especially as she was young and nervous and rather small, while Tom was very tall. She recalled Tom asking her where she was from and she replied Basingstoke so from then on, Tom always called her Miss Basingstoke!

When asked about recent and current work, Matthew discussed playing the priest in the 1978 play by Alan Ayckbourn - Joking Apart. He summarised the events of the story and how the characters develop throughout, describing it as a "great play, a very funny, dark play" and his enthusiasm and eloquence was very evident throughout.

They were asked if the actors ever met each other

socially. Sarah hadn't seen Matthew since they left the series in the early 1980s, but she saw Janet Fielding occasionally. She noted that one reason she enjoyed conventions was as it gave her an opportunity to meet up with actors she had worked with. She was looking forward to seeing Mark Strickson later, as she hadn't seen him for a while, the last time being when she was in Australia with her husband.

Sylvester was very funny and entertaining on stage. He sat on the sofa, then promptly fell off and the audience loved it all, of course. He was asked about the 1996 TV Movie and explained things as he saw them. "They were making a film for America and at the same time trying to drop things in for the Doctor Who fans" like the jelly babies, so he felt its heart was in the right place, but as nothing had happened after film, the fans became more critical of it in hindsight.

Sophie joined Sylv on stage partway through and they bantered and joked well together. Sylv commented that he did the last so many series of Jigsaw, then was in the last couple of series of Eureka – then he went into Doctor Who and it ended!

Manopticon was held just after the General Election (won by Tony Blair's Labour) so politics came up in several of the panels, with Sylvester calling himself a 'federalist' and Richard Franklin saying he was a member of the Referendum Party.

Matthew Waterhouse was asked whether he would do a party political broadcast. He said he probably would, but only a Labour one. When an audience member quipped "As Adric?", Matthew's eyes lit up. "Oh yes!" suggesting Adric's fate could be a warning as to what might happen under a Tory government!

It was a good day; both Dad and I enjoyed ourselves and certainly intended to go to more Doctor Who events in the future.

Dad meets Tom Baker at Manopticon
and I meet Sylvester McCoy

Mid-May brought two more Doctor Who autographs in the mail, as both Sarah Sutton and Sophie Aldred sent me signed photos. In July, I received letters from Colin and Lis Sladen, who also included a signed postcard. My friend Trevor had met her at a convention only three days previously and passed on my letter to her.

In June, I rang Bill at Llangollen (who organised Travellers in Time) and booked a place for the July weekend, as Colin Baker was going to be there again.

In the meantime, I discovered my old school friend Katie Robinson knew Colin too. I think she had been one of the kids in the pantomime previously and knew him from that. She said he was lovely and had kept in touch with her since.

The next Llangollen weekend began at 2pm on Friday 25th July. I was going on my own this time so had to make the train journey from Lincoln to Ruabon alone. I had a phobia of travelling and found it quite difficult, but got there and had an amazing time.

John Nathan-Turner and Gary Downie were there once more and Colin Baker. Rebecca Thornhill (from the Doctor Who stage play The Ultimate Adventure) had been planned as a guest originally, but she couldn't make it, so the director Carole Todd stepped in instead. David Roden (the writer of Dimensions in Time) was also in attendance.

One of the first organized events was a Doctor Who themed treasure hunt, which was a great 'ice breaker', which allowed you to get to know the other fans. This was fun and one of the items we had to find was John Nathan-Turner! He was sat in the pub and we had to collect an autograph from him as one of our 'treasures'.

I ended up pairing with a man called Nik for the treasure hunt, who told me he was 22 years old, from Bristol and was a postman. I said "Oh, my husband's a postman too!" Not the greatest of chat-up lines to the man destined to become my husband a few years later!

I sat near Colin Baker during the Friday evening meal and the conversation turned to the Teletubbies, which were a big thing at the time and with both of us having young daughters, we had seen it more times than we cared to count! I also gave Colin a paperweight I had bought him as a present.

We all played Charades on the Friday evening, which was great fun with all the celebrity guests being involved too. I seem to recall it became quite competitive!

I got on better with JNT and Gary Downie this time. They seemed to need to get to know you before they fully relaxed and trusted you. I was particularly fond of John, but ended up having a few issues with Gary over the time I knew him. He was rather fond of a bitchy aside! Carole Todd was lovely, but I really did not get on with David Roden at all, who I found rude and offensive.

This time, one of the activities was a mock audition in front of John and Carole. We were auditioning for the roles of Crystal, Jason and Carl from The Ultimate Adventure. I can't remember many details now, but it was nerve-wracking but fun and I can't have been too bad, as I won the part of Crystal. Nik was given the role of Jason too. There was some talk of doing a performance of a scene or two, but I think we unfortunately ran out of time.

The Saturday was spent away on a trip as we visited some of the locations used in Doctor Who. We climbed up some bleak Welsh hills to see the places used in The Five Doctors. This included the ruins of the castle at Plas Brondanw, where the Fifth Doctor, Turlough and Tegan walk round in the episode. Colin, John, Gary, Carole and David posed in front of it for us to take photos.

We also travelled to Portmeirion, where the Masque of Mandragora was filmed (as well as being the home of the cult TV series The Prisoner). Portmeirion was quite picturesque if a tad gaudy with its gold paint and many statues.

It was pouring with rain all the time and it was tiring trekking round the woods and up hills. It felt like an outward bound course at some times! Colin seemed exhausted at times and sat at the bottom of the hill for a while to rest.

On the Saturday night, we had a good evening of dancing and karaoke. I sang Big Spender with Gary Downie and a couple of others. I also danced the Macarena and Timewarp with Gary who – not surprisingly, given his background – was a very good dancer.

Later on in the evening, Gary offered to do free Tarot readings for anyone who wanted one. I had never had this done before (nor since), but as I was going through a difficult time with my marriage and feeling rather stressed, I thought I would give it a go and see what Gary said. I hadn't told him anything much about my relationship, but his reading was very accurate – conflict at home, big arguments about money and so on – and I did follow some of the advice he gave me.

There were twenty-two of us who went to the weekend and on the Sunday, we were all presented with autographed graduation-type scrolls to commemorate it. We had plenty of opportunity to get other autographs and photos besides, as it was an open policy and all of it was free. It was the most fantastic experience for fans being so close to the stars and mingling them with them for the entire weekend.

After coming home from Llangollen, Nik and I kept in touch and it soon became obvious we were falling in love. I told my husband who didn't seem to care too much, as our marriage had been hanging on by a thread for a year or so. He soon moved out and Nik became my boyfriend, driving up from Bristol to Lincolnshire to see me as often as he could.

The next Doctor Who event I went to was Event One in Weston-super-Mare in August. Again, it was complicated to arrange with needing people to look after the kids and sorting out travel arrangements. I had to get up at 4am and got a taxi to Lincoln, a train to Birmingham then met up with a man called Paul (who was a Llangollen regular) and he drove me to the convention.

Event One was a two-day convention organised by Ian Burgess, which was held at the Winter Gardens on Weston's Sea Front. The guests on the first day were Colin Baker, Nicola Bryant, Nicholas Courtney and Elisabeth Sladen with her daughter Sadie Miller, who was 12 or 14 at the time (depending if you believe Wikipedia or IMDb).

Everyone was very friendly. Lis was lovely and Sadie took a photo of me with her Mum. Colin remembered me (of course) and was very sweet. It was the first time I had met Nick Courtney and he was great too, but I was most impressed by Nicola, who told Colin I had been to see her at the Theatre Royal in Lincoln and recalled my daughter Leigh-Ann being a fan too.

I got lots of items signed, including a 10" x 8" photo of

Colin cuddling me in the TARDIS console at the Doctor Who exhibition in Llangollen. He wrote "For my friend, Karen. As ever! Colin Baker" and this remains one of my favourite signed photos because of that lovely inscription.

Nik picked me up after the convention finished on the Saturday and I stayed at his parents' house, which was the first time they had met me. He attended the event with me on the Sunday where the special guests were Colin, Nick and Lis again (this time with both Sadie and Brian Miller, Lis' husband) and Carole Ann Ford, who was the only one I didn't get to meet. David J. Howe was there too, as were Colin's wife Marion and their four daughters.

It was another good day, though I felt a bit ill from not eating enough. I found travelling and eating in public very stressful, so usually didn't bother to eat much.

While I was in the autograph session, I took a lovely photo of Lis and her daughter Sadie together. I later got this reprinted and enlarged to give to her as a gift.

On August 31st, Princess Diana died. I was at home with the kids, but Nik was in the Isle of Man at the Recorder convention, celebrating the Patrick Troughton era with Frazer Hines, Anneke Wills, Michael Craze and Deborah Watling. Wendy Padbury had been due to go, but couldn't manage it in the end.

Nik passed my letters on to Frazer, Anneke, Michael and Debbie and got their autographs for me. As Wendy wasn't there, he bought me a signed photo of her in the auction for £12. During September, I got a letter and signed photo from Frazer in the post, a signed photo from Deborah Watling and a signed postcard and note from Michael Craze.

In September, Nik and I went to Panopticon in Coventry. This was one of the biggest annual conventions and featured an impressive line-up of guests – four Doctors (Tom Baker, Peter Davison, Colin Baker and Sylvester McCoy), eight companions (Elisabeth Sladen, Louise Jameson, Mark Strickson, Sarah Sutton, Deborah Watling, Anneke Wills, John Leeson and Sophie Aldred) plus Nicholas Courtney, Jacqueline Pearce, Michael Sheard, Peter Miles, Kevin Davies, Mike Tucker, Peter Tuddenham, Gary Russell, Rebecca Levene, Mat Irvine, John Nathan-Turner and Gary Downie.

We were at Coventry the whole weekend from Friday afternoon to Sunday evening. During that time, we managed to meet most of the celebrities there. I had learned from my mistakes at Manopticon in May and wasn't going to let those autographs elude me this time!

It gave us plenty of time to meet old friends and new. Going to different conventions and signings mean you tend to bump into the same people and it is easy to make friends. We saw Jason Thomas (Jay) at this one. Nik knew him from the Recorder convention on the Isle of Man, but this was probably the first time I met him. My daughter Leigh-Ann was a big fan of the Teletubbies and being in London, Jay managed to get us a cuddly Laa-Laa for her, which we hadn't been able to find locally. We have met some great people through attending events like these and Jay is one of the best.

I met Tom Baker at his signing on the Saturday and found him very charming again. He autographed a postcard for my daughters Leigh-Ann and Emilia, commenting that he liked their names and spellings. I asked to have a photo taken with him and he was very obliging. I said could I put my arm round him for the picture and he was happy to agree. Despite Tom's reputation as being a bit scary, I have never had anything but wonderful experiences of meeting him.

I only saw Colin Baker on the Saturday autograph session, though he was around on the Sunday too. He had received my letter and asked how things were at home (with my ex now living elsewhere) and how my children were doing. He said he was taking Marion out to celebrate their 15th wedding anniversary, so wouldn't be at the Celebrity Dinner.

I met Sylvester McCoy socially on the Saturday night and at the signing on the Sunday. Again, I found him to be a lovely man. He had an obvious rapport with Sophie and she sat on his knee at the bar for some of the time. I seem to remember she had recently married Vince Henderson and had brought her wedding photos to pass around and show everyone.

The fourth Doctor I met was Peter Davison. He was signing with Mark Strickson on the Sunday and I was much more interested in chatting to Mark, so ended up almost ignoring Peter – oops! I did get a book and postcard signed by him, but when I had a photo taken with both of them, I was standing much closer to Mark and Peter commented he had 'gatecrashed' the picture! When I had it developed, Mark and I are looking happy and Peter looks decidedly moody!

Meeting Peter Davison and Mark Strickson
and (below) Sophie Aldred

Nik and I went to the Celebrity Dinner – my first at a big convention. There were two celebrities per table and they swapped round after each course, so each table had six guests with them in total. Our table had Rebecca Levene (author and editor of the Virgin New Adventures) and John Leeson with us during the starters. I found John to be very intelligent, kind and sweet. I was talking to him about my children and he said I was "a mum in a million and one" which was very sweet of him.

During the main course, we had the rather strange Peter Miles on our table (who I found scarier in real life than Nyder ever was!) and the wonderful Nick Courtney. I talked to Nick about Lincoln and he said he had done a play there in 1977 with Kate O'Mara and Peter Byrne and that Lincoln Cathedral was his favourite.

I had Mark Strickson for Dessert. What more could a girl want?! Those pale blue eyes looking straight at you... As always, he was wonderful company, energetic and eloquent. We were talking about the Llangollen weekends and he said Wendy Padbury (who had done the Travellers in Time weekend that March) was his agent at Evans and Reiss. He told me he hadn't received the letter I had sent him via Manopticon, but always replies to fan mail. He ended up giving me his home address and telephone number!

After the meal, Nik took a photo of me and Mark together. Mark put both arms around me for the photo, which was rather nice too and thankfully the photo turned out well, so I was able to enlarge it and put it in a frame.

The other highlight of the weekend was meeting Lis Sladen on the Sunday. We chatted during the signing session and I told her I had got the photo of her and Sadie enlarged as a gift. She said she was really touched and became a bit emotional, saying she didn't have any recent pictures of the two of them together. We were talking so much to me that she apologised to the other fans waiting, explaining she was "just talking to my friend" – a lovely moment.

The day after, she wrote me a thank you note on the back of a postcard, saying she appreciated my thoughtfulness. As ever, I appreciated hers.

Tom Baker began promoting his book in September so was appearing on television. I saw him on This Morning on September 30th. Nik met him at the book signing he did in Bristol in October.

October brought more replies in the mail. John Nathan-Turner sent me a letter, while Rebecca Thornhill (who had been scheduled to go to Llangollen but hadn't been able to) sent me a letter and a large signed photo.

I had been trying to see if I could get Mark Strickson as a guest for one of the Llangollen weekends, as I had spoken to him about it at the Panopticon Celebrity Dinner and he had sounded interested. I had written to George Smith (the manager at the Dapol Factory in Llangollen) and JNT about it and had tried ringing Mark to let him know, but had to speak to his wife as he was busy "doing an edit" and couldn't be disturbed.

A couple of weeks later, he rang me back! He was as friendly as usual and even spoke to my daughter Leigh-Ann, who was thrilled and went off to watch Resurrection of the Daleks again afterwards! I asked him if he could meet us that weekend as we were travelling to Cardiff (and Mark was based in Bristol), but he was unable to, as he was busy editing his film on kangaroos.

On October 18th, Leigh-Ann (who had just turned seven a few days earlier) and I travelled from Lincoln to Bristol on the train, then met up with Nik who drove us to Cardiff. The event was called A Day in the Life of Elisabeth Sladen. It was an interview, question and answer session and autographs.

Leigh-Ann loved meeting Lis. I have some cute photos of

them together. Lis remembered me and gave me a kiss at the end of the event.

Leigh-Ann meets Lis Sladen in Cardiff

My third Travellers in Time weekend in Llangollen took place in November. It was our biggest family trip yet – me, Nik, my Dad and Leigh-Ann. The special guests this time were Colin Baker and Deborah Watling, with JNT and Gary Downie in attendance as always. David Roden and Andrew Beech (one of the organisers of the Panopticon conventions) were there too. There were about forty of us altogether.

The Friday began with a quiz (where I came third!) then Dad and Leigh-Ann did the treasure hunt. By this time, we had made friends with quite a few of the other fans who we had met at several events over the year, so it was good to catch up with everyone.

There was a talk by John Nathan-Turner in the hotel at 6pm on the Friday and he had brought some models from the series to show us – a working model of a Haemavore (which looked a bit like a large eye on a neck!) and the bronze headdress, known as the Six Faces of Delusion, which was worn in Snakedance. John posed wearing this for a few photos too.

This was followed by Debbie Watling's panel, before dinner at the hotel. Debs wore a stunning outfit – a black tight lacy top with a sparkly gold and black jacket with black trousers.

During this session, she was asked for her fondest memory of Patrick Troughton which caused her to pause for a long time. With a tear in her eye, she described Pat as "a wonderful man, made me laugh a lot" and noted he was "very attentive, he cared, he was a very caring person" who looked after her during the freezing cold location shoots, putting his arm round her and getting her a cup of coffee.

She said when there was a crowd of people, Pat always felt he had to perform and entertain everyone, but that she enjoyed her time with him most when it was quieter, having a drink with him in the bar after work. She said she cherished her "private memories" of him and emphasised "I liked the *man*."

Saturday's entertainment included Gary Downie's talk and Colin Baker's Question and Answer session. Colin's talk was fascinating. He explained the differences between filming then (in the 1980s) and now, including how filming used to have to stop at a certain time, whereas now you just keep going until you have finished.

He said there was an incredible pressure on actors and complained how nowadays, there just isn't time to rehearse anymore. When he was the Doctor, his week's schedule would be something like a read-through on Wednesday morning, blocking it on Wednesday afternoon, then rehearsing and learning it. The producer would check it, then you would get one day off (probably Sunday) before it was back to the studio to film it on the Tuesday and Wednesday.

He said you still get a week to do it now, but you shoot from the first day, so you have to learn all your script before turning up (so you are "learning words in a vacuum") and he doesn't enjoy it so much. The rehearsal period was ideal for learning the part and how to interact with your fellow actors, but now the BBC gives its floors over to accountants rather than creative departments.

He had filmed both The Bill and Casualty recently and noted these were different, as they have their own permanent sets. He said Casualty's set in Bristol is a fully-equipped hospital ward, properly built but with some temporary walls to get the cameras in. The Bill is the same kind of thing with permanent sets of a police station, hospital and so on. It is worth constructing these as they are long-running series, but otherwise anything like the old studios they had has ceased to exist. He missed the days when the BBC used to be run by programme makers like Shaun Sutton who understood it. These days, it was all about administrators who cared about budgets and figures over quality.

His part in The Bill took him three days to film – one day shooting a scene on the hospital set, one day to shoot eight scenes in a house, then a third day on his other set. He explained how there were three colour-coded teams on The Bill, making three different episodes at any time. He compared the organisation behind this to being "like organising timetables for schools."

He said he had been pleased to meet up with the

producer Chris Clough on The Bill, as they had worked together on Trial of a Time Lord in 1986, when Chris was the director.

He was asked if he would play the part of the Doctor again. "Get it right this time, you mean?" he laughed, in response. He said he would love to do it for fun, as "it was a ball, it was great fun to do" saying he'd love to get John Nathan-Turner and "the old team back" but noting philosophically "you've got to go forwards not backwards."

He did wish he had been able to do a full story with the Brigadier though and wished he'd been able to complete the cancelled Auton story. He also felt his Doctor hadn't had a proper "thumping good" Master story and regretted that missed opportunity.

Asking if he had read any of the new Sixth Doctor novels, Colin said the "mean streak" in him meant he didn't want to pay £4.99 for a book about his character with his image on the front, complaining that "I believe my face helps sell that book". This led to a bit of a rant about the unfairness of the artist or photographer owning the rights to an image, rather than the actor depicted. He acknowledged JNT had helped with the issue during his tenure, insisting the actors were included in any deal made at the time.

On a lighter note, Colin was asked where he envisaged the 35th anniversary of Doctor Who going. "After the 34th?" he suggested, laughing, before commenting that the 50th anniversary would be more significant and important. He said he was amazed Doctor Who Magazine was still going. He read and enjoyed it, but had expected it to have a limited lifespan once the programme itself had finished.

Questioned about conventions, he said he had several coming up, including one in 1999 for which he had been booked in 1996! He commented that he didn't *not* enjoy conventions, but would prefer to be with his children and take them to the cinema than being at a Doctor Who event – but that he does enjoy conventions when he's there.

41

He mentioned having lots of pets and that the latest addition to the menagerie were a couple of horses. Three of his daughters had been having riding lessons at £7.50 per half hour and someone suggested it would be cheaper to buy their own, so a farmer friend had offered him one. He was insistent it did *not* work out cheaper. ("Heaven help us! Don't do it!") He said his wife loves horses, so the pecking order in the household was now "horses, kids, cats, dogs, friends, neighbours, me."

There was a bonfire party and firework display on the Saturday evening, hosted at Argoed Hall, the home of David Boyle, the owner of Dapol. He was a very kind and generous man and put on an amazing firework display which included fireworks in the shape of a Dalek and K9!

There was a karaoke again, which was always fun and this time, I managed to avoid any reckless attempts at a solo effort! Five of the Doctor Who fans (Peter, Paul, Peter, Paul and Kent) had formed a kind of gang through these weekends, calling themselves the Titters (using the acronym from Travellers in Time). It became something of a tradition for them to sing karaoke with JNT and Gary Downie. On this evening, they were joined by another fan Amy (who, like me, idolised Colin) and the eight of them wore matching burgundy polo shirts with the Doctor Who Experience logo on them.

They sang Hi Ho Silver Lining and Calendar Girl. Any bit of music, Gary had to move to! John usually took lead vocals with the others doing backing vocals. He was such a good sport! He didn't have perfect pitch at all, but he did pretty well.

Leigh-Ann and I sang Summer Nights with Colin Baker performing the male vocals. Colin stood on one side, while us girls (me, Leigh-Ann, Keeta and Amy) shared the other microphone, singing the girl's parts. After we finished, Colin came over and chivalrously kissed Leigh-Ann's hand.

Leigh-Ann had long dark bunches and was wearing a

green and white dress. At one point in the evening, Gary Downie took her onto the dance floor and they bopped along to the Spice Girls. Gary was really going for it - ever the showman! – while Leigh-Ann seemed to be a bit tired, as though she was only doing it to humour him!

Colin did a wonderful solo rendition of the Connie Francis hit Who's Sorry Now? Admittedly it was late in the evening and most of the fans had been drinking, but one particularly obnoxious fan – a guy called Martin, who dressed as the Master – began howling while Colin was singing. I was outraged and turned round in my seat to tell him off. How ignorant and rude! It seemed to annoy Colin too as at one point, he did say "Stop talking when I'm singing!" (though in mock severe tones). I know Colin doesn't hit every single note perfectly, but he's always entertaining and can carry a tune pretty well. This song always reminds me of Colin now, when I hear it.

All four of the celebs then joined with the Titters to sing Vic and Bob's version of Dizzy. However, Debs complained she didn't know it, Colin gave up and ambled off to one side, so JNT took over lead vocals. All the time, Gary was happily dancing and doing actions to the words; he was never happier than when he was performing.

In the end, Debbie gave up trying to follow the words and instead began dancing too, letting the others sing. She started acting, prancing around and having a laugh, but finally disappeared stage left.

Later on, she really came into her own though. She sang Big Spender accompanied by Andrew Beech and the guys from the Doctor Who Appreciation Society (DWAS). Once she got into it and let herself go, she was very good. She started pouting and acting, urging "Quiet boys, quiet boys!" to the DWAS lot, while Gary continued dancing in the background. I believe it must have been this experience which led to her famous number at Weston-super-Mare in 1998...

Colin then returned with another solo – The House of the Rising Sun. The far too vocal 'Master' Martin yelled out "Earplugs are available!" but Colin continued unabashed and gave a very good performance again.

The highlight of the evening though was watching Andrew Beech and Deborah Watling singing the Elton John and Kiki Dee classic Don't Go Breaking My Heart. The music seemed to go on forever and Debs got a bit fed up, so she ended up saying the lines and acting them by the end of it, instead of singing. She had a good voice though and it was pleasant on the ears.

There was a very cleverly thought out version of an old Saturday night TV classic to entertain us that evening – The (Re) Generation Game. It was hosted by Andrew Beech and Keeta (who organised the weekends with Bill) who were sporting matching red jackets. Dad and I were one of the couples, but didn't do very well. It was great fun though. One task involved Debbie dancing the Macarena while her team-mate had to sing relevant words to do with Doctor Who.

The most memorable game was where one partner had to completely cover the other one in white sheets and toilet roll to become a Mummy! Colin Baker had to dress up a fan nicknamed Sarge, which he did with gusto. The other partnership saw Deborah Watling being wrapped up as a mummy, with extra assistance from Gary Downie and Andrew Beech! Seeing little Debs totally covered in white was a rare sight and a unique photo opportunity!

Our main trip was on the Saturday when we went to the Ironbridge Hill museum and Blists Hill, the Victorian town used for location filming in The Mark of the Rani.

We watched the video of Mark of the Rani in the coach, while Colin himself added interesting comments, before we reached the place it was filmed. Rather surreal, but an unforgettable experience.

The 1985 story used the scenery to great affect. As it was set around the time of the Industrial Revolution, the location was ideal as that is the period reconstructed by the working community of Blists Hill, part of the museum's attraction.

This is a whole village set in that era – a bank where you can change your money into old currency, then various shops where you can spend them. The old industries are well represented too, so you can walk along the paths and really get a taste of how things used to be. There is a plumber's, confectioner's shop, chemist, pub, cobbler's shop, printing shop and a draper, for example.

They had huge pigs which walked around freely, so Leigh-Ann sat on the back of one to pose for a photo with Colin. The pig obviously got bored and started to walk away, leaving Leigh-Ann toppling backwards! Luckily Colin was quick to react and caught her.

There was a photo session with Colin and Debs, both wrapped up in their winter coats. Little Debs was probably a foot smaller than Colin, but she stood on top of an old piece of farm machinery, so the height difference wasn't so extreme. When we went over to stand with them for a photo, Collin lifted Leigh-Ann up and she sat on his arm with her arm around his neck for balance.

All the celebrities were very good with her. Gary Downie 'borrowed' her special toy George the penguin and they all looked out for her and made sure she was entertained all weekend.

Leigh-Ann made a Davros at the Dapol factory and later on when she did her Craft badge at Brownies, she used her model to pass one of the sections. I bet not many other Brownies had a Doctor Who figure they had made!

There was another tour round the Doctor Who

exhibition, a pub lunch and the usual signings and photo opportunities. I spent the Friday evening meal with Debs and had three meals sitting with Colin, so we had plenty of time to chat as well.

I had a bit of a falling out with Colin at one point though. We let Leigh-Ann stay up late as it was a holiday for her and one evening, she was sleeping across a couple of chairs in the room we were all in. He made a few snide comments about us being wrong to allow her to do that, suggesting we were being selfish and should have taken her off to bed earlier. Colin can be very opinionated if he feels he is right and while usually I agree with his views, I didn't in this case. Leigh-Ann was fine of course and it didn't sour my opinion of Colin for too long.

Overall it was another great weekend at Llangollen with many lasting happy memories for all of us.

John Nathan-Turner

Deborah Watling

Our next event was in Sheffield on a very foggy day in late November. It was a long day for Nik to as he had been up at 4am to do his postal round, then had driven from Bristol to Lincoln after work, then from my house to Sheffield!

Mark signing in Sheffield

This was An Afternoon with Mark Strickson at the Sheffield Hallam University and it was run by a group called The Watchers. There was an interview, a Question and Answer session then a long queue to get autographs. It was worth waiting for though, as he gave everyone enough time to have a chat, take photos and get things signed.

At Panopticon, the Doctor Who artist Martin Geraghty had been doing drawings for charity and I had asked him to do headshots of my three favourite Doctor Who men – Colin Baker, Matthew Waterhouse and Mark Strickson. So I got this signed by Mark at Sheffield, hastily adding it was 'in reverse order' as Mark is the third drawing. He jokily said "I should hope so!" in reply.

His interview was very interesting. ITV were scheduled to show his documentaries on snakes and crocodiles in January 1998 and he was finishing work on the kangaroos film. He commented he would love to make a film on wolves, because he loves dogs. (I later bought him a wolves calendar and posted it off to him as a Christmas present!)

The Mark Strickson event was our last Doctor Who one for 1997, but what a year it had been. Until March, I had never been to a convention or signing and here I was, knowing some of the actors quite well and regularly travelling all over the country to meet them. I had been to Manchester, Coventry, Sheffield, Cardiff, Weston-super-Mare and had spent three very enjoyable weekends in Llangollen.

Chapter Three
Moving On – And Out

The first Doctor Who related event I went to in 1998 was a trip to see Frazer Hines in pantomime. He was in Beauty and the Beast at the Theatre Royal, Lincoln with Kim Hartman from 'Allo 'Allo. This one didn't stand out in the way Dick Whittington had the previous year and we didn't get chance to meet Frazer either, so it was slightly disappointing.

January 1998 saw Louise Jameson's first appearance in EastEnders, which I had watched since the start but had even more reason to now. She played Rosa di Marco, the mother of four children in an Italian family and was in the soap until August 2000.

I kept in touch with Keeta from the Travellers in Time events and she rang me in early February to say they were hoping to organise another Llangollen weekend with Katy Manning and maybe Peter Davison. I definitely wanted to go, so started thinking about raising the money (again!) and childcare arrangements.

A couple of weeks later, Keeta told Nik that Mark Strickson was due to do a Llangollen weekend in March. I was pleased as I had been pushing for him to do one, but I was also annoyed as I wouldn't be able to get the money to go.

One thing that cheered me up was a rather bizarre television appearance from Colin Baker. He was on Noel's House Party with Lionel Blair and Michael Elphick and they all got gunged!

I was then watching GMTV one morning and they

announced Colin was going to be on Lorraine Live between 8:35 and 9am. We didn't have a VCR that recorded (only one that just played tapes) so I had to get all the kids ready and rush round to my Dad's house to tape it! He was being interviewed with Robert Powell to promote their tour of Kind Hearts and Coronets, which would be coming to Lincoln in April.

By March, Keeta had confirmed Katy Manning for the April weekend, but said it wouldn't be Peter after all and she was trying to organise one or two others. (I had my fingers crossed for Mark or Colin, of course!)

Ian Burgess rang me too. He organised the conventions in Weston-super-Mare and we had exchanged a few letters and phone calls following the first event. Anthony Ainley was going to be the big attraction at the 1998 event! I agreed to pass on a letter to Katy from Ian when I met her. I think he was hoping to do some work with her in the future. He also got Mark Strickson lined up to guest at Event One and wrote to tell me, as he knew I would be pleased!

As March went on, the plans for Llangollen seemed to be changing quickly, with lots of problems amongst the organising team. Keeta rang to say the whole weekend events were hanging in the balance, as Katy might not be coming and John Nathan-Turner had walked out because he was fed up of guests not turning up!

She finally confirmed on March 31st that the April weekend would be on after all! Katy Manning would be there with one other special guest, but no JNT or Gary Downie. A couple of days later, I got a letter stating that the April weekend was indeed going ahead, but it would be the last one they did. Another phone call with Keeta on the 9th informed me the second special guest would be John Leeson. I was pleased to hear that, as he seemed a really pleasant man when I'd met him the year before.

I was receiving Colin Baker newsletters from Michael Sibley during this time, who ran Colin's fan club. These were black and white A4 newsletters which contained information about his plays, TV work and personal appearances.

Kind Hearts and Coronets played at Lincoln from April 20th to 25th. I went to see it on the first night with my fellow theatre-loving friend Lesley. This was the stage adaptation by Giles Croft. Colin was playing all the d'Ascoynes (the roles Alec Guinness played in the famous film version from 1949) while Robert Powell was Louis Mazzini (the Dennis Price part). It took me a while to get into the style of it with people playing different parts and ages in the past, present and future, but once I did, I enjoyed it and it was very cleverly done.

We met Colin again afterwards and had a good chat about the Llangollen weekends finishing and Katy Manning being scheduled to do the next one. He asked what we thought to the play, how my kids were and how my relationship was going with Nik. He was very friendly, gave me a hug and a kiss on both cheeks and I had a photo taken with him for my increasing collection.

The final Llangollen weekend was April 24th to 26th and I went with Nik (who was still living in Bristol, so we were having a long-distance relationship) and my Dad. There were 38 people at this one, including Andrew Beech and Andrew Eaton from DWAS, Keeta and Bill who organised it, Katy Manning, John Leeson and the film-maker Keith Barnfather from Reeltime Pictures, who was working on a video of Katy.

The Friday we arrived there, the itinerary included a trip round the Dapol factory, a Doctor Who quiz (which Nik won) and model making session, an hour's panel with Keith Barnfather and then a magician who performed after our meal.

We all had fun at the model making where we had to make model K9s out of clay – and then John Leeson judged which one was the best! It was just like being back at school, big tables covered with newspaper and constructing carefully shaped blobs of clay into something vaguely dog-like. Mine even came with accessories as I also made a bowl and a bone!

John called up each table in turn and we had to bring our models up for inspection. He described my effort as being "a very long K9, rather like a Dachshund" but was impressed with my accessories, pointing out it had "a bowl *marked* K9 and a bone – brilliant!" Nik's creation seemed to have John short of words for a while, but he finally quipped "Let's not tinker with perfection. Very good." while he said Dad's model was "absolutely brilliant. Not K9 but wonderful! Yes, highly amusing!" I don't think any of our models won.

In the Dapol factory, each Travellers in Time weekend included the chance to make your own Doctor Who model of some kind. You went through the whole factory process, helped all the way by the staff who worked there. This included putting the parts together and spray-painting them. After your model was dried, the guest stars would autograph the cardboard insert and the whole thing would be sealed in its plastic packaging. These made great souvenirs and we ended up with quite a collection, mainly Daleks of varying colours.

At the April 1998 weekend, I made a blue and gold Dalek and a blue K9. The Dalek was quite easy to make (under strict supervision from the experts, of course!) but the K9 was really fiddly and difficult with lots of small parts to negotiate. The celebrities made their own too and Katy seemed to be there for ages working on her K9 and in the end, she needed quite a bit of assistance from the factory staff.

The evening's entertainment was very disappointing with

magician Steve Cooil and comedian Dave Milton failing to impress. In fact, the comedian was so appalling, we left early. At least that meant we didn't stay up late on the Friday night and could catch up on some sleep. These weekends were tiring!

On Saturday morning, we all went on a tour of Plas Newydd with Katy Manning and John Leeson. This was where the Ladies of Llangollen - Lady Eleanor Butler and Miss Sarah Ponsonby - lived together from 1780 to 1829. They adapted their small cottage into a Gothic style by adding stained glass windows and oak carvings, so it is a fascinating place to visit and is now surrounded by beautifully landscaped gardens.

Although the place itself is well worth a visit at any time, our trip was definitely enhanced by being there with Katy Manning! She was the perfect guide for this tour with her brilliant readings, accents and characterisations. It was one of the funniest days of sightseeing I've ever had!

Afterwards, we had plenty of opportunity to photograph the stars in the grounds. Katy looked gorgeous posing against a tree in her leather flying jacket with her hair in a ponytail, while John posed serenely sitting on a large rock.

Before the photo session, Katy applied lip balm, jokingly complaining "I thought this was a weekend of no glamour!" Of course, she never looked less than stunning the entire time!

She recalled how she had done loads of press calls while she was in Doctor Who, as the series was at its peak in popularity at the time. She said people would often stop her in the street and say things like "Woo-hoo, where's your TARDIS?" and she was usually in the newspapers a couple of times a week then.

I took about eighty photos and this was way before digital cameras, so they cost me £30 to get developed later! Some of the photos were lovely, especially one I took at the hotel where Katy is lying across my Dad and Nik. She was a really good laugh and great company all weekend.

After we had been to Plas Newydd, we went to Llangollen Wharf for a horse-drawn canal boat trip through the Dee Valley. The boat trip itself was slow, relaxing and a tad boring, but Katy was entertaining as usual. She had her hair in bunches and fell in love with the horse. She has a wonderful way with animals and an obvious connection with them.

Afterwards, we went back to the Doctor Who Experience to look round and the celebrities signed autographs in the TARDIS Console and posed for photos. In the exhibition, John Leeson posed with the model of K9, happily agreeing to do a few phrases in K9's voice for the eager fans. (Well, it was my Dad mainly! "Do the voice, John!")

Back at the hotel afterwards, John Leeson did a Question

and Answer session, followed by an hour with Katy Manning doing a talk and answering our questions.

Saturday evening, we had our meal in the hotel and I sat next to Keith Barnfather. We got on well and chatted about lots of things including the Myth Makers videos he made. I always find it difficult eating when I am nervous, so these meals can be quite stressful but I found him very easy to talk to and he was really kind and sympathetic about my issues. He said the celebrities just want to be treated as normal and that Katy had been anxiously asking him if everyone liked her!

After eating, we had a karaoke but it was a bit disappointing as Katy and John didn't really join in. Colin Baker and Deborah Watling had thrown themselves into the karaoke at previous Llangollen weekends and had been brilliantly entertaining. Andrew Beech was very vocal though and Katy urged the singers on, conducting, dancing, head-banging and wiggling her bum in time to the music! We all managed to have fun anyway, as I stayed up until 2am!

I sat with Katy at the breakfast in the hotel on Sunday morning. She was very relaxed and friendly and we had a very good chat, without her usual accents and acting. My daughter Leigh-Ann liked Katy, especially as they share a birthday (October 14th) and had been sorry she couldn't come to the weekend to meet her. I told Katy this and later on, she gave me a handwritten letter to give to Leigh-Ann when I got home. A very sweet gesture.

After breakfast, it was back to the Dapol factory. There was a final autograph session in the TARDIS Console Room at the exhibition and a photo opportunity watching Katy and John sign the Café walls, alongside the signatures of the other Doctor Who guests that had visited before. Then our weekend was over and it had been another great one with brilliant people.

John Leeson was really lovely and my Dad got on with him very well too. They are around the same age and have similar aged children, as John said he had a child three years younger than me. I found John to be very intelligent, kind and considerate and a good listener, though he also seemed quite shy and not very outgoing. He worked well as a guest with Katy, as she is really outgoing and bubbly, so they made a good pairing for the event.

Andrew Beech generated plenty of laughs. He was messing about a lot, flirting with the men and even playing with my Dad's hair at one point! He also told me Matthew Waterhouse is gay, which I didn't know until then. (As I fancied Matthew at the time, this was a bit disappointing.) There was another side to Andrew though and sometimes he could be rather bitchy and didn't know when playful teasing had crossed the line and turned into insults and offensive comments. He realised he had gone too far with me at one point and when I got his autograph at the end, he signed my itinerary with 'Many apologies'.

But it was a small blip which didn't spoil the weekend too much. This was the last Llangollen weekend ever organised, so it was good to end on a great one. The Dapol factory stopped making the models in 2002 (after the BBC decided not to renew their licence) and the Doctor Who exhibition closed in 2003. If only they had hung on another couple of years, things could have been so different.

Anyway, it was back to normal life for me, Nik and my Dad. I went back to being a housewife and mother in a Lincolnshire village and things were fairly mundane for a while. I still read Doctor Who novels and watched the episodes on video, of course and I still looked out for any mention of the stars from the programme.

One of the television appearances I saw at the end of April was Bonnie Langford on This Morning. She was interviewed and then performed songs from the musical Sweet Charity. She turned up on Terry Wogan's BBC1 one show on June 1st as well. She was playing Charity Hope Valentine at the Victoria Palace theatre in 1998 and was promoting the musical. I would have loved to have seen her in it, but at the time I avoided travelling to London.

I did go to the theatre in Lincoln though. Lesley, Nik and I went to see Spider's Web on June 4th. It is an Agatha Christie play from 1954 and this tour featured two Doctor Who actors – Frazer Hines as the detective Inspector Lord and Richard Franklin as the justice of the peace Sir Rowland Delahaye – as well as Jill Greenacre from The Brittas Empire, who played Clarissa Hailsham-Brown in the play.

It was excellent; I enjoyed the murder mystery aspect and it was a well-acted, entertaining and funny play. I got to meet Frazer afterwards and he signed a birthday card for my Dad, my Companions book and the video cover for Tomb of the Cybermen. I didn't get to meet Richard though. One of the other actors, David Callister (who played Jeremy Warrender) said Richard had an early rehearsal the next morning, so had probably gone back to his digs as he was tired. I'd written a letter to Richard, so gave it to David to pass on.

The next day, Nik, the kids and I travelled to Bristol in the car. Nik's parents looked after the little ones, while we took Leigh-Ann to the Event One convention in Weston-super-Mare. This was another two-day event organised by Ian Burgess and was held at the Playhouse Theatre, which was a great venue for it.

On the Saturday, the guests were Anthony Ainley (headlining), Nicola Bryant and Nicholas Courtney. This day wasn't quite as good as the Sunday, as I felt tired and had a headache, but I still enjoyed it.

Nicholas Courtney's interview threw up a few new interesting facts. He said he was a Christian, that he knew French, Italian and Latin and his favourite film was A Man for All Seasons. He stated his favourite Doctor Who stories were Inferno and The Daemons.

This was the first time I had met Anthony Ainley, my only previous experience being the bitchy criticisms Gary Downie used to level at him at Llangollen. This may have clouded my judgement somewhat, as initially I thought he was a bit strange (enigmatic might be a better word) and wasn't quite sure what I felt about him.

He was very critical of John Nathan-Turner (not much of a surprise), which I wasn't keen on, as I had a lot of respect for JNT myself. But Anthony was very interesting and clever, though he did come across as rather shy, nervous and slightly evasive at times. A fascinating character.

In his talk, he commented that he shared a birthday with both Sophie Aldred and Sylvester McCoy (August 20th), making them all the star sign Leo. He said he loved Ceefaxing, Countdown, Carol Vorderman, Larry King and Anita Ekberg, but hated JNT (!) and the Australian actress Coral Browne (who was married to Vincent Price).

He said he was a non-smoker and loved his sport, especially cricket and rugby (which he referred to as 'rugger') and enjoyed playing tennis, but found it boring to watch.

Leigh-Ann and I meet Anthony Ainley

I had been shopping in Lincoln beforehand and had bought a Lincoln Cathedral glass for Nick Courtney (as he'd told me he liked the cathedral) and I got a black domed Lincoln Cathedral clock for Anthony Ainley which I felt fitted in well with his role as the Master.

When I gave him the clock at Weston, he was grateful and surprised. I had Leigh-Ann with me and he said she was "beautiful" and gave us both free signed photos, instead of charging us the £4 each. So, a man of contrasts, hard to work out.

Nick liked his glass too. I gave him the gift at the bar and he was really pleased and gave me a kiss. He told me his wife was also called Karen. He was a real sweetheart as always.

Nicola Bryant was lovely too and attentive to Leigh-Ann who was a fan. I took a nice photo of the two of them together and she signed several things too, taking time to carefully dedicate them 'To Karen and Nik and Leigh-Ann'.

In her talk, she also said she was a Christian like Nick

Courtney. Her favourite classic films were Waterloo Bridge and Brief Encounter. She had been filming Parting Shots with Peter Davison and described its infamous director Michael Winner as an 'ogre'.

The Sunday seemed better organised; it flowed well and kept everyone interested. The guests on this day were Nicholas Courtney (the only one to do both days), Deborah Watling, Sarah Sutton and Mark Strickson.

The stage talks brought out some interesting little facts about each of the actors. Deborah Watling said she liked listening to Elgar and walking up hills in Malvern.

Sarah Sutton's husband is called Mike, she didn't have Sky TV at the time of the convention and had only been nineteen when she had got the part of Nyssa, two years after she had starred in Moon Stallion.

She likes cricket, drinks tea (not coffee) and had recently been in a television programme called 999, where her character had given birth.

She likes Cybermen and said her favourite Doctor Who stories were Black Orchid and Earthshock. She said the latter was nicknamed 'Boom Boom Waterhouse' and 'Matt Finish'! This led on to her mentioning Lalla Ward's dislike of Matthew Waterhouse, which is legendary by now anyway.

Mark Strickson's interview was the one I took most notice of – him being my current 'crush'! I noted he had blond hair, blue eyes and was 5' 10" tall. After I came round from my swoon, I then listened to him telling the audience how he enjoys cooking, gardening, walking the dog and brewing his own beer (though he also drinks herbal tea). He had been working on more wildlife documentaries with Steve Irwin and was soon going to be visiting Botswana to look for lizards! (As you do.)

The highlight of the whole weekend – apart from the gorgeous Mark! - was the cabaret! Being in a theatre, Ian Burgess made good use of the stage and Deborah Watling performed an amazing song and dance routine to Big Spender. She wore a black sequinned leotard showing off her great figure and she was amazing! She got a standing ovation and had to do an encore! A wonderful moment.

Sarah Sutton was sweet again and very good with Leigh-Ann and gave her a signed photo free. They had advertising boards at the event for each actor and I bought Sarah's board for £4 (which I believe went to charity) and she signed it for me. I also had a photo taken with her and Mark Strickson.

I asked Mark if he had received the wolves calendar I sent him and he said he had. Sarah had stayed at his house the night before and he explained to her it was the calendar he had up on his kitchen wall.

Deborah Watling remembered me, Nik and Leigh-Ann from the Llangollen weekend in 1997. She was very friendly again. I asked her if she had received the letter I had sent her, but she said she hadn't and that she would have replied if she'd got it.

I also had a good chat with the writer David J. Howe, who's a nice bloke and we talked to Ian Burgess too, who asked us how we thought it had gone and who we would like to see at future events.

Just four days after meeting him, I received a lovely letter from Anthony Ainley thanking me for "the most splendid clock" and saying it was "a delight" to meet us. I replied and we became quite regular correspondents for the next three years or so.

I heard from him twice more in 1998 and one of them was written on the back of a shooting script for Trial of a Time Lord from July 1st 1986. (It was a night shoot at Gladstone Pottery Museum and filming began at 7pm for Colin Baker, Bonnie Langford, Tony Selby and Geoffrey Hughes with Anthony Ainley beginning at 11pm.)

I had sent him a birthday card and he included a Jon

Pertwee trading card, writing – "For your kindnesses I'm sending you a picture of the one they call the Doctor – you are welcome to it." He concluded the letter "Yours mundanely, Anthony Ainley."

I also heard from Nick Courtney who sent a lovely long handwritten letter thanking me for the glass we gave him and enclosing two signed photos.

Our next event was with Nicholas Courtney too, in Sheffield on June 27th. He did a talk for around an hour and was as interesting as usual. He said William Hartnell was 'bigoted' and 'too right wing' for his liking, but he had only good things to say about the other actors who had played the role.

There was a raffle afterwards, then autographs which were limited to a generous four per person. He remembered us (Well, it had only been three weeks!), he recalled my name and once Leigh-Ann said hers, he remembered the spelling. He asked if I had received his letter and said he used the glass and was very pleased with it. I gave him a mug this time and he promised to use it for his tea!

July brought a wonderful letter in the post from Tom Baker! This was at least the third letter I had written to him, but the only one to receive a reply. I hadn't been sure how to begin the letter as 'Dear Tom' sounded too informal and 'Mr. Baker' too formal, so I had decided on 'Dear Tom Baker'. So he began my letter 'Dear Karen Inskip', ha!

It was a fabulous letter, handwritten in beautifully cursive script and remains one of my most treasured possessions. He thanked me for my "marvellously eloquent letter" and said "I shall keep it carefully to comfort me in the twilight". Ahh. You gotta love him.

Colin Baker and Michael Jayston at Longleat

August 2nd was the annual Doctor Who day at Longleat so I went there with Nik, his Mum (also a long-time Doctor Who fan) and my three daughters aged 7, 5 and 2 years old. At the time, Longleat had a permanent Doctor Who exhibition, which was a big attraction. (It closed in 2003.) There were also plenty of other attractions for the children to enjoy, so they didn't get too bored.

Colin Baker and Michael Jayston were the special guests at the 1998 Doctor Who event. It was a really hot day and we had to queue for two hours. The actors had a gazebo to shade them from the sun somewhat, but we didn't have any protection and I seem to remember we ended up sunburnt. Despite that, the day was good fun though and especially when we all met them and got their autographs. I took a photo of Colin with my daughters Leigh-Ann and Emilia.

We bought the video of Where On Earth Is Katy Manning? while we were at Longleat. This was the one Keith Barnfather had been filming at Llangollen and both

Nik and I were in it, as well as my Dad. It is a 55-minute film following Katy over a period of ten weeks as she attends various events and meets some Doctor Who stars and plenty of fans.

A few days later, we went to a dog rescue centre near to where I lived and found a Jack Russell cross Chihuahua we wanted to adopt. We called her Katy, after Ms. Manning who I always associate with her love of animals.

Later that month, we (me, the kids and pets) moved from Lincolnshire to Bristol to begin living with Nik.

On October 3rd and 4th, it was the Panopticon convention at the Leofric Hotel in Coventry, which Nik and I went to. It was a particularly special convention for us, as we got engaged there on the Saturday during the Celebrity Dinner!

The guests at Panopticon included two Doctors – Colin Baker and Sylvester McCoy, four companions – Sophie Aldred, Peter Purves, Wendy Padbury and Mary Tamm, plus Nicholas Courtney, Richard Franklin and a mixture of writers, guest stars and others – Lisa Bowerman, John Nathan-Turner, Gary Downie, Nick Briggs, Bruce Purchase, Donald Pickering, Andrew Cartmel, Brian Blessed, Bob Baker, Chris Boucher, Terrance Dicks and Delia Derbyshire.

Initially, I was rather disappointed with the guest list, especially as Anthony Ainley and Caroline John had pulled out. The celebrities I really want to see usually fall into two categories – those I know quite well and want to see again (Colin, Mark Strickson, Lis Sladen, Anthony Ainley, John Leeson) and those I have never met yet. At least Peter Purves and Mary Tamm ticked this second box.

Nik was in his element though as he is fascinated by hearing from the authors and backstage crew. Talking to other fans though, it seemed I was not alone in finding this particular Panopticon somewhat disappointing.

The Saturday began with a panel with Lisa Bowerman and Sophie Aldred being interviewed on stage together. I took an instant like to Lisa and when I met her later, found her to be very friendly and sweet with a very infectious warmth and enthusiasm about her.

While Lisa was signing the audios, Nick Briggs was talking to her, so I got his autograph too. He was very charismatic and had an expressive face. He was looking very cool in his leather jacket too!

Sophie Aldred is always great value and looked very pretty. I was pleased to see she wasn't as thin as she had been the previous year too. Her interview was interesting. I found out she likes reading Jane Austen and non-fiction rather than sci-fi. She had recently travelled to ex-Soviet Georgia to do a theatre festival and had been to Australia with Vince in November 1997.

She was filming ten episodes of Words and Pictures and two country programmes for regional television. She said she can relate well to the countryside, as she used to regularly holiday in Norfolk as a child. She loves The Archers and is a member of their family thanks to Terry Molloy (Davros). She also added to the countryside image by commenting that she wears a pair of green wellies which Keith Barnfather had bought for her!

The next panel was Peter Purves. He came across as a bit cold and stand-offish, both during the interview and when I met him later at the autograph session. The people sat at his table for the celebrity dinner said he was more relaxed then, but from what I saw of him, I can't say I felt any warmth towards him. He also didn't allow anyone to take photos of him during the signing.

His interview was good though and it was interesting seeing his reactions to the clips they showed on the screen, including his first viewing of his Morton Dill character in The Chase. He said he got on very well with William Hartnell and they used to eat out together regularly, with

Hartnell always insisting on paying. But Peter agreed Hartnell often gave people a hard time, sometimes only talking to a guest actor if the script required it, but ignoring them completely off set!

Peter said that after he finished working on Doctor Who, he only had three weeks' work in the next eighteen months and he sounded very resentful about this. He kept the Trilogic Game from Doctor Who but eventually threw it away, believing it to be unlucky. The next day, he got the Blue Peter job!

He talked about his background in the theatre too, saying he did Repertory with the Renaissance Theatre Company in Barrow-in-Furness, where they performed 96 plays in two years!

After Peter Purves, it was Colin Baker's time on the stage. He was filming Sunburn with Michelle Collins in Cyprus and flew over in-between filming, so he left after only a couple of hours. His panel was good though. He said he used to share a flat with David Troughton and was best man at his wedding. He was also good friends with Vere Lorimer (the director/producer of Blake's 7) who shared Colin's birthday and had recently died.

Colin said he 'marginally' prefers television and film work to theatre. He said his daughter Bindy was a fan of Star Wars, but had recently started watching Doctor Who, which he was pleased about.

I didn't get to meet Colin this time, because I decided to stay in the Main Hall to see Brian Blessed's talk. Nik met Colin at the autograph session though and he sent me his best wishes.

Brian Blessed was the special guest and was absolutely brilliant – entertaining, interesting, funny and passionate about Doctor Who! He had me in hysterics at times, then moved me almost to tears by reciting a beautiful speech from Man of La Mancha. He was fantastic; I could have happily listened to him all day! Unfortunately, I didn't get chance to meet him, but I only heard good things about him from those that did.

The afternoon session in the Main Hall got all technical for a few hours, so I couldn't raise much enthusiasm for them really. It was Andrew Cartmel and John Nathan-Turner then a rather dull music workshop with Mark Ayres, Roger Limb, Malcolm Clarke and the rather strange Delia Derbyshire.

There was a slightly more interesting panel with Bob Baker and Paul Mark Tams, who were talking about the new K9 project they were involved in. They let us watch the show reel they have done, which – rather unfortunately – was met with some mirth and derision from the audience. Admittedly, the sight of 'K9 with Aqua-Lung' and 'K9 with Heavy Artillery' was… er … something new, but surely any project like this should be supported by Doctor Who fans.

Tom Baker was voicing the K9 character and the new design for K9 was cute and modern, but not too far from the original concept. They couldn't show us the actual model though, as they were waiting for the funding to make one! It would be over a decade before these plans came to any kind of fruition.

Chris Boucher and Terrance Dicks were up next and were fairly interesting. By this time though, I was getting a bit tired and my thoughts kept wandering, comparing Dicks to a Sontaran, while worrying about Boucher looking far too thin and frail.

Finally, we had a return to the actors (Hurray!) and a UNIT panel with the wonderful Nick Courtney and the equally charming Richard Franklin. Richard said he was in the process of moving to Brighton and would be in panto at the Elgiva Theatre that coming festive season, doing Aladdin which was produced by JNT and choreographed by Gary Downie.

He said he saw himself as an actor, writer and director.

He stood for James Goldsmith's Referendum Party at the last General Election. He used to own a giant maggot from the Green Death but gave it to a young fan, though he regrets that in hindsight.

Nick was also doing pantomime and was going to be in Dick Whittington at the Mill Field Theatre in Edmonton. He said he wanted to direct in the theatre. He owns the original 'swagger stick' from Doctor Who and recommended Patrick McNee's autobiography Blind in One Ear as a great read.

Nick Courtney and John Nathan-Turner signing

Richard Franklin

There endeth the day's entertainment at around 6:30pm and we had to dash back to our hotel then to get changed for the Celebrity Dinner which began at 7:30pm. We had told Andrew Eaton (of DWAS) about our intention to get engaged at the meal and his eyes had lit up, so we were very nervous and trying not to think about it, but he ended up being too busy to organise anything (finding sausages for Sylvester's cabaret act, for one thing!) and it went as we had hoped really.

We sat on the same table as Andrew Beech and Nick Courtney and chatted with them and other fans, while trying to eat. (Never my forte, even without the additional nerves!) After the coffee, we told Andrew about our engagement and he leapt into action!

The room was full of 120 people (including Peter Purves, Wendy Padbury, Bob Baker, Mark Ayres, Nick Courtney, Bruce Purchase, Sylvester McCoy and Lisa Bowerman) and he told them all to be quiet, then said there was going to be a 'Jerry Springer moment'. He announced us and said thee was something Nik wanted to ask me. So we stood in the middle of the room, Nik got down on one knee and asked (very shakily) "Karen, will you marry me, please?" and I squeaked out a 'yes'. He tried to put the ring on my finger and I had to help him as he was shaking so much. Then everyone applauded, we escaped to our table and drank wine to steady our nerves!

When we had recovered, quite a few people came over to congratulate us and to see the ring. They included Sylvester McCoy, who was exhausted as he had been filming links for BBC Choice all day.

The next day, we had people coming up to offer their best wishes too. Bruce Purchase (the Pirate Captain in The Pirate Planet) kept asking "How's the wedding going?" in his deep booming voice, Wendy Padbury admitted she'd had a tear in her eye during the proposal and we had congratulations from Lisa Bowerman, Nick Courtney and JNT as well.

After the Celebrity Dinner, Saturday's entertainment continued with a showing of the brilliant video of 'The Few Doctors' – a great parody by Dominitemporal Services starring various DWAS members (including Andrew Beech as the Fifth Doctor) and cameos from Peter Miles and JNT. It was very funny and we ended up buying the video. (It is available in four parts on YouTube.)

There was also a cabaret, where some of the Doctor Who alumni performed various little turns, some more successful than others. We had artist Alistair Pearson reciting a witty ditty, Wendy Padbury reading out a poem about knickers, Gary Downie doing a kind of striptease, Bob Baker playing sax, also JNT and Lisa Bowerman doing a magic illusion.

One of the funniest acts involved Sylvester McCoy, Andrew Beech, a length of black knicker elastic and a pack of sausages. The most memorable act for me was Richard

Franklin who performed a reading of a 'Confession of What Mike Yates and Jo Grant Really Got Up To' (a bit long-winded but not bad) then sang in a pink dress and feather boa!

By the Sunday, Nik and I were down to our last £6 so ate well at breakfast! We got to the Leofric in good time and were sat in the Main Hall ready for the first panel. As I had found the first day rather disappointing, I vowed to aim for lots of autographs and photos for the second. I managed this successfully and felt this day was much more productive and enjoyable.

I watched Wendy Padbury's interview on stage, then Nik remained in the Main Hall for the Ghostlight panel with Sophie Aldred, John Nathan-Turner, Mark Ayres and others, while I went off to the seminar room.

Richard Franklin was holding a talk for around ten people in the smaller room, so I wanted to be sure of getting a place and got there early. As I hadn't met him at Manopticon in 1997 (when I was new to conventions and didn't understand the techniques of queuing!) and then narrowly missed meeting him in Lincoln after Spider's Web, I was determined not to let him slip through my fingers again!

I got a seat right at the front and asked lots of questions so consequently he directed most of his answers to me, so it almost felt like we were having a one-to-one chat! He is a fascinating man, extremely intelligent and passionate about lots of things. He talked about politics, philosophy, history and the morality of Doctor Who amongst other topics. When I mentioned getting engaged, he made me tell everyone in the room about it!

It was really good, the best part of the entire convention (except for the proposal, of course)! The hour flew by and afterwards, some of us stayed back to get autographs. I also bought Richard a cup of tea, which he was grateful for, spending my last 35p! (Not that he knew that, of course.) I asked for a contact address and he gave me his agent's.

I saw him around a few times after that and he was always very pleasant and attentive. He posed for a photo with me too and I later introduced him to Nik too.

After the seminar, I spent the next three hours queuing, though it was worth it as I got the autographs I wanted and as always, I met some interesting people while waiting on the stairs.

The first signing I went to was Lisa Bowerman, Sophie Aldred, Wendy Padbury and Bruce Purchase. Wendy remembered me (and my Dad) from the first Llangollen weekend back in March the previous year. She still looked just as youthful and her hair was blonder, which suited her.

The next autograph session featured Nick Courtney, John Nathan-Turner, Donald Pickering (who was in Time and the Rani and The Faceless Ones) and Mary Tamm.

I was particularly looking forward to meeting Mary and she was very pretty, but sadly I didn't like her much. She came across as rather snooty, full of false smiles and she appeared rather bored with it all.

She had some beautiful photos for sale, but I was completely skint by then. There was one black and white 10x8 I fell in love with, so I asked if it was available to order via mail order. She sighed and asked "Well, can't you get it now?" I explained I had run out of money, so she said (sighing again) "Well, I suppose you could get one from my agent, but he'd probably only send a small one. I only bring these with me to appearances."

Finally, she decided to give me the photo for free, but told me 'not to tell anyone or they'll all want one.' While I appreciated the gesture, surely it could have been done with more grace. It was only a £3 photo after all. Still, I told her about our engagement and she did write 'Happy engagement!' on it. But no, I wasn't impressed with Mary Tamm.

After all the queuing, it was time to go back to the Main Hall to meet up with Nik. We watched the end of the video interview with Patrick Troughton from Panopticon 1985, which was on the big screen. It was interesting and moving too. I liked Pat; I wish I had been able to meet him.

The last panel of the day was Mary Tamm and Bruce Purchase together, then there was a brief video montage followed by everyone coming back onto the stage for farewells.

It had been a tiring weekend and in some respects disappointing, but we enjoyed it overall and it was a very special experience to get engaged the way we did.

Our final Doctor Who event for 1998 was a Thames River Cruise in Reading on November 15th with William Russell, Cynthia Grenville and Bruce Purchase. It was fun with us all on a boat, meaning we had a good opportunity to chat to the actors, take photos and get their autographs. They were all very nice and I enjoyed meeting William for the first time. There was a full size Dalek on the trip too and William Russell happily posed for photos with it. He was an affable chap, if a bit reserved and quiet. (William, not the Dalek!)

Bruce Purchase was his usual self – anything but reserved and quiet! His booming voice could easily be heard all round the boat, so we always knew where he was. He remembered us from Panopticon too and I think he asked when we were getting married.

Leigh-Ann meets William Russell

The last couple of months brought some good mail too. As well as signed photos from Peter Purves, Caroline John and Bonnie Langford, I also received two letters and a signed photo from Jackie Lane. She had retired from acting many years ago and rarely appeared at Doctor Who events, so it was quite difficult to get her autograph.

We adopted a cat from the local rescue centre around this time. He was a scary looking feline with a constant frowning expression, but was very gentle really. We called him Delgado, which seemed a fitting name.

1998 finished with the sad death of Michael Craze in December, aged just 56. Nik had met him and really liked him. Although I hadn't met him, I was a fan too and it was very sad news.

Chapter Four
(Time and) Space 1999

1999 began with some good Doctor Who related mail, as I received another letter from Anthony Ainley (this time accompanied by a UNIT trading card) and Jackie Lane wrote again, returning my video cover of The Ark signed as promised. We exchanged a few letters and she was very kind and obliging. She wrote that she didn't do conventions due to stage fright and I believe this was why her acting career was curtailed.

Our first Doctor Who meeting of the year was once again Colin Baker. He was in pantomime at the Wyvern Theatre, Swindon. He was playing the Dame in Jack and the Beanstalk. He has been the Dame many times in his career and whilst I find him much more attractive *not* dressed in women's clothing, I must admit he does seem to revel in the chance to go really over the top! He is fantastic at comedy and the Dame role gives him plenty of chances for double entendres and saucy humour.

In this particular pantomime, the cast also included Rod Burton, Jane Tucker and Freddy Marks – otherwise known as Rod, Jane and Freddy from Rainbow, which was one of my favourite programmes as a child growing up in the 1970s.

While we were waiting outside the stage door after the show had ended, Jane Tucker came out and I went to get her autograph. She greeted me, my husband and children as old friends, which seemed very nice. Then we realised she really did think we *were* old friends and that she knew us! It was quite embarrassing as we didn't want to lie, but the whole thing was really awkward. In the end, we sort of made the right noises and just hoped she'd go away! Thankfully she did, then Colin came out to say hello. He had two of his daughters with him – Lucy who was then thirteen and Bindy who was ten.

One of the missing episodes turned up in January too – Episode 1 of The Crusade! (I am still optimistic they will all turn up at some point.) 1960s Who featured again this month as I got to see episodes one to three of The Tenth Planet for the first time. Our Welsh friends Trevor and Ben (who we had met at Llangollen) came over to see us and brought the video tape with them. I remember being impressed with it and finding the early Cybermen voices fascinating (if a tad comic).

In March, I was pleased to see Katy Manning again, though this time only on TV! She was on the Ruby Wax show with her friend Liza Minnelli.

On, March 6th, we went to A Day in the Life of Sophie Aldred at the University of Wales in Cardiff, which was fun and Leigh-Ann loved meeting Sophie! This was an event organised by Neil Goodman and a non-profit organisation called TIMELESS. It was a one day event which began at 11am and finished at 5pm. It included an interview with Sophie, question and answer session, photo opportunities and autograph signing. There was also a charity raffle and Sophie decided to donate the money to the Terence Higgins Trust.

That year's Red Nose Day for Comic Relief brought a brand new television episode of Doctor Who – albeit in a comedy fashion! Doctor Who and the Curse of Fatal Death was written by Steven Moffat (You may have heard of him…) and starred several incarnations of the Doctor – most notably the wonderfully versatile Rowan Atkinson, but also Richard E. Grant, Jim Broadbent, Hugh Grant and (Controversy!) Joanna Lumley. It was very funny and brilliantly written. Jonathan Pryce played the Master and was great entertainment value too. This was the last new episode to be made until Rose in 2005.

Our first convention of the year was April 10th and 11th when me, Nik and Leigh-Ann (now aged 8 ½) went to Battlefield II, which was held at the Rougemont Hotel in Exeter. Neither Michael Sheard nor Peter Purves could attend in the end, but Sophie Aldred was added to the list. Joining her as the stars of the event were Colin Baker, Peter Davison, Elisabeth Sladen, Nicola Bryant, Nicholas Courtney, Donald Tosh and Keith Jayne.

The events began at 10am on both days, but people were usually around by about 9am. We left around 6pm, though there was a cabaret and celebrity dinner on the Saturday night which we chose not to go to.

It was a mixed convention really, as there were plenty of great bits but I had many complaints too. The event was organised by Mark O'Grady who marched round the hotel with a consistently blank expression on his face, as if he was planning a military coup rather than a pleasant Doctor Who convention.

The main thing that annoyed me was his new rule of attendees having to pay for autographs. At all previous events, they had been free. Here we were given six tickets of varying shades which entitled us to one free autograph each from Colin, Peter, Nicola, Lis, Sophie and Nick. All other autographs were charged at £1 a time.

Poor Keith Jayne and Donald Tosh spent hours waiting in the signing rooms with periods of very little to do, as all of their signatures had to be paid for. Nik queued up for twenty minutes to meet Donald Tosh, only to be informed by the stewards that he couldn't ask him to sign anything unless he paid £1 for the pleasure!

After talking to various other attendees there about this rule and discovering that we all shared the same view, I approached Mark O'Grady. After waiting patiently for a few minutes before he finally acknowledged my existence, I calmly and politely explained my grievances. His reply was simply that I should note down any complaints I had on the questionnaire, then he turned away. I persisted, stating that I was voicing the concerns of many of the people there, to which he reiterated his suggestion about the questionnaire, before asking if I was enjoying myself! Argghhhh!

But besides O'Grady and the autograph costs, everything else was fine and the stewards and officials fulfilled their roles well. Gary Russell and Gary Gillatt did a particularly excellent job in announcing and interviewing, while being very approachable and friendly throughout.

There were several things happening at once over the weekend with the panels on stage in the main hall (Devonshire Ballroom), someone in the photo studio (Chatsworth Room) then celebs signing in the Compton Room and the Burlington Room. We flitted between the interviews and autograph sessions. The photo studio was quite expensive with it costing £12 to be photographed with one star, £15 with two. Professional photographer Robin Prichard took them, but even so, it was a bit out of our budget!

Saturday's events began at 10:15am with Colin Baker's interview on stage. He was as entertaining as ever and always provides value for money. He had been recording the new Doctor Who audio The Sirens of Time with Peter and Sylvester, so was telling us about that.

Some titbits I picked up from his interview were that his daughter Bindy had seen all of his Doctor Who videos by that point, he is against fox hunting, he drives everywhere and he lives 35 miles from London.

Elisabeth Sladen was on stage next and looked great, younger than ever! She always dresses elegantly and comes across as a real lady. She had taken a year off doing conventions so I hadn't seen her since October 1997.

After this, we went to collect some autographs. We met Sophie first and she remembered us – perhaps not surprisingly, since it was only about five weeks since we had met her in Cardiff. Most people remembered Leigh-Ann too

81

as little girls rarely seemed to go to Doctor Who conventions in those days, with most attendees being males of all ages.

We had a chat with Sophie and gave her some chocolates. We tried to give our favourite celebs small gifts when we could to show we appreciated them. Sophie was lovely as ever, very warm and natural. Sometimes with autograph queues, you can feel part of a production line, but Sophie always makes time to chat to fans, gives you her complete attention and seems genuinely interested in talking to everyone.

We met Colin afterwards and gave him some chocolates too, which he was pleased with. We had a good chat and on one photo, he signed it "To Karen – an OLD friend! Colin Baker."

We then went to listen to Sophie being interviewed on

stage. Leigh-Ann was pleased to hear Sophie was going to be a character called Minnie the Mini Magician in the next series of 'Zzzap!' on Children's ITV, as she enjoyed that programme.

Other titbits we learned from her talk included her favourite story being The Curse of Fenric, her favourite enemy being the Cybermen and her favourite television programmes including Friends and Spank the Pony. She studied A-levels in English, French and Music.

One of the highlights of the Saturday for me was meeting Gary Russell – writer, former editor of Doctor Who Magazine and producer of the Doctor Who audio adventures. I had seen him at events before, but this time I looked at him in a different light. I had found an old piece of schoolwork from 1978 in which I said my ambition was to meet the Famous Five. I had been a huge fan of the television series and had only recently realised that the Gary Russell who had played Dick (Make up your own jokes!) was the same one involved with Doctor Who!

I told him about this and he autographed a book for me. He was interested in the piece of schoolwork, so I brought that in to show him on the Sunday, along with a Famous Five puzzle book which had him on the cover. We had quite a long conversation and he told me what had happened to the other cast members. He was still in touch with Marcus Harris (who played Julian) and Jennifer Thanisch (Anne).

But next up on stage on the Saturday afternoon were the 1960s writer and script editor Donald Tosh along with Nicholas Courtney. Some of what Donald was saying was fascinating – what William Hartnell was like, about the famous Christmas episode The Feast of Steven, why they killed off Katarina in The Daleks' Masterplan and so on - and he is obviously a very well-read and intelligent man. But other parts of the talk went on a bit too long and this wasn't helped by the uncharismatic and dull Jeremy Bentham conducting the interview.

At one point, Nick Courtney fell asleep on stage and both Nik and I were worried he might have died! It was funny afterwards, but my heart skipped a beat at the time and it was only when we saw his chest rise and his eyes flicker, that we could see the humour in it!

The next person we met at the autograph sessions was Elisabeth Sladen. Although hadn't seen her for a year and a half, she still remembered me and about the photo I took of her and Sadie. She was warm and friendly, signing one photo 'Love once again, Lis xxx'. We gave her a box of clotted cream fudge and it was all going magnificently, until she said "Oh, I can see your tummy! How lovely!"

Now, I had put on about 1 ½ stone since I had last seen her, but I wasn't pregnant! It was really awkward as I didn't want to make Lis look silly or feel embarrassed, so I just muttered some kind of neutral 'mmmm' noise and moved on. Needless to say, Nik thought this was hilarious and kept reminding me of it all weekend.

Lis was only there on the Saturday. On the Sunday, Peter Davison and Nicola Bryant arrived and were joined by Colin, Sophie and Nick again.

The morning began with Peter Davison's panel on stage, which Nik watched while Leigh-Ann and I went to the autograph rooms to see Sophie and Nick Courtney. Virtually everyone else was watching Peter on stage, so we were able to spend quite a long time chatting with them. I told Sophie about Lis thinking I was pregnant and after insisting I wasn't at all fat, she told me how some woman she knew had seen her in a baggy jumper and congratulated her on being pregnant! I had no idea how anyone could mistake Sophie for being pregnant, as she had a flat tummy to die for, but it was comforting anyway and made me feel a bit better about myself.

We also had a conversation about birthdays as I asked her to sign a birthday card for my daughter Emilia, who was just about to turn six. Leigh-Ann said she shared Katy Manning's birthday and Sophie asked her if she was a Scorpio, so we talked about star signs and birthdays. Sophie said her mother shares her birthday, her brother's is on Hallowe'en and her father's is on New Year's Eve, so she said they are easy dates to remember and they always have big celebrations.

I took a photo of Leigh-Ann and Sophie together. After being discouraged from asking the stars to pose for photos on the Saturday, I decided to make up for it on the Sunday and took photos of Leigh-Ann with all the guests! The stars themselves were happy to pose for photos and very accommodating; it had been the stewards who decided it shouldn't be allowed.

We talked to Nick Courtney for a while too, as we were

the only people in the room again. I asked if he had received the Christmas card I had sent him from me and Nik and he said "Yes, but you're not *that* Karen, are you?" When I said I was, he commented that I had changed my hair as it used to be short, which was correct. I said he'd shaved his beard off since I had seen him, but that I liked it. He said he had only got rid of it for a part and would be growing it back later.

He remembered meeting Leigh-Ann before and even recalled how to spell her name right again! She loved it when they recognised her. When Nicola Bryant left the hotel at the end of Sunday's events, she said "Bye, Leigh-Ann!" as she went past.

We went to watch the end of Peter Davison's interview, which was entertaining and he was very witty. We discovered his favourite story is The Caves of Androzani and his favourite enemy are the Cybermen. He also said he was born in Streatham, South London but he moved to Woking in Surrey when he was ten years old.

Then we went to join the queue for his autograph, which was our longest wait (along with the queue for Nicola later) and stretched up two levels of the hotel!

Having previously found Peter rather sullen and seemingly resentful of being 'forced' to sign autographs and be sociable, I was prepared to give him a second chance to impress me. He managed a slight smile for Leigh-Ann and a forced one when I asked him to pose for a photo, but otherwise appeared uncomfortable and unhappy. We gave him a birthday card (He shares Emilia's birthday) and he just said something like "I'm doing well for those" before putting it behind him with the others he had received.

So off we went. I was by now convinced that I didn't like him. But the story wasn't over, by any means…

Peter Davison with a Dalek (above)

Back to the main hall to watch Nicola and Colin together on stage. Both Nik and I commented that Nicola seemed to be reciting well-rehearsed lines a lot of the time, as though she was acting a part. It was particularly obvious with her being paired up with Colin, who is excellent at talking about anything and comes across as very natural and happy in this kind of situation.

Peter Davison and Keith Jayne were on stage together too. Keith's Doctor Who connection came from a role in The Awakening but he had also been in Stig of the Dump and Murphy's Mob. It was another interesting and enjoyable interview.

After that, we queued to meet Nicola, who remembered me from Lincoln two years earlier. She was friendly, especially to Leigh-Ann, but each time I saw her – and especially as we got to know Sophie better, who was very natural – I couldn't help thinking that, at the time, she approached conventions as an acting job. "Today, I'm going to be Nicola Bryant from Doctor Who…"

The final panel was the two Doctors one with Colin and Peter on stage. Fans shouted out a word or name (Bonnie Langford, Daleks, carrot juice, etc.) which Gary Gillatt or Gary Russell would then turn into a question. This worked very well and was something clever and original, which everyone seemed to enjoy.

During this session, a trailer for The Sirens of Time audio was played and the general consensus was that it was brilliant! Hearing the old familiar theme tune, then having Colin, Peter and Sylv playing the Doctor again – yes, there was a magic about it!

It was towards the end of this panel that Leigh-Ann and I needed the loo (as you do). As we were washing our hands in the Ladies, we met Elizabeth Morton (Peter Davison's girlfriend and an actress). They had earlier mentioned that she was expecting Peter's baby in July, so I congratulated her and she was very sweet.

We came out of the Ladies to see another fan talking to Elizabeth and getting her autograph. I didn't have any paper with me, but waited to ask if I could take her photo. As Leigh-Ann and I were waiting, Peter Davison walked along the corridor! He seemed a completely different man from how he had been in the autograph queue and was happy, smiling and very pleasant. He said hello to us and I asked if I could take a photo of him with Leigh-Ann. He stood next to her, only to realise that the big height difference between them meant that a close up was pretty difficult, so he squatted down next to Leigh-Ann, so they were the same height.

After that, I took Elizabeth's photo, then they left the hotel, while Leigh-Ann and I returned to the hall. But that short meeting changed my perception of Peter Davison forever!

We saw Colin again briefly and said goodbye to him, before we went to the car park and then back home to Bristol.

Our next big event was Time After Time at the Playhouse in Weston-super-Mare on June 12th and 13th. It was disappointing as we couldn't go to both days and Nik was unable to do either, so I ended up just going on the Sunday with Leigh-Ann, our friend Pierre and his son Louis, who was also eight years old.

When we arrived, we were sorry to discover the two

guests we had been most interested in – Louise Jameson and Caroline John – had only been attending on the Saturday. Not the most auspicious of starts. Still, at least we had three old favourites there – Colin Baker, Deborah Watling and Wendy Padbury.

I was especially glad to meet the wonderfully charming Wendy again, particularly as she was planning to retire from the convention circuit at that time. She is one of the real ladies around and one of the most genuine.

We found seats on the front row and the day began with Colin talking on stage for an hour or so, then answering questions. For once, I even asked one! He seems to be working well, as he said he was going to play a motor biking vicar in Dangerfield, the Head of MI6 in The Waiting Game and would be in panto in High Wycombe with Gary Wilmot and Brian Cant.

After he came off stage, we had a word with him and gave him a birthday card and two bottles of Spanish Rioja, his favourite red wine, as it was only five days since his birthday.

Debbie was on stage next, being interviewed by Simon Gerrard, the day's compere. She told some interesting anecdotes, making even the ones I'd heard before entertaining.

Then it was time to collect autographs from the three guests. The queue was very good-natured but took longer than anticipated and eventually, Colin and Wendy had to walk down the queue themselves, signing as they went along. They still took time to chat to everyone though and were relaxed and friendly.

One of the funniest bits of the day happened in this queue. Trevor was there again, so we spent a lot of time with him. As well as being one of the loveliest guys I've ever met, he was inclined to be, shall we say, rather vocal. You certainly knew when he was in the room and all the actors knew him by name.

So that day, my daughter Leigh-Ann bet Trevor that he couldn't keep quiet for the whole day – a very difficult challenge for him! The rest of the people in the queue were taking an interest in the bet and it became a bit of a talking point. (Though not for Trevor, ha ha!)

The deal was that if he kept silent all day, Leigh-Ann would buy him a Dapol Millennium Dalek and if he spoke, he had to buy her one. Well, after a record twenty minutes or so of silence, I was getting a bit worried! Then Colin came along the queue and we told him what was happening. So he reached Trevor, who thrust out his book for signing, still saying nothing. Colin refused to sign, saying how rude he was for not asking properly! This happened another two or three times, until Trevor cracked. "Oh, bugger you, Colin!" he complained, laughing – and Leigh-Ann became one Millennium Dalek richer!

Wendy was pleased to see me again and to meet Leigh-Ann for the first time. She signed a few things for us and confirmed this would be her last convention, at least for a couple of years.

Back on stage, it was the auction next, although this part of proceedings seemed much slower than the first part and we spent a lot of time just sitting around, waiting for something to happen.

The auction itself was good, though I felt that too many items were offered as one lot with bids starting at £10. I only had £8 left by this point and would have happily used it to buy something smaller, but didn't have enough to bid. If I'd had the money, I would have loved the EastEnders script signed by Louise Jameson.

This was followed by the panel with the Soul's Ark team – Colin, Wendy, actor Mark Danbury and Ian Burgess, who was the mastermind behind the project. It was a sci-fi/horror film featuring Carole Ann Ford alongside Colin and Wendy. This kind of idea – using Doctor Who actors to create new drama – had been done successfully by Bill

Baggs and his team, where Colin had played a recurring Doctor-type character called The Stranger. These video releases helped feed the need from fans and give the actors some slightly different roles to work with.

The Soul's Ark panel at the convention suffered somewhat though because the video wasn't available to buy at the time and one surprise element involving Mark Danbury's character had to be talked around, so as not to spoil it! The project sounded exciting and professional though and I did buy it once it was released.

The climax to Time After Time was an hour long show. This was the best part of the whole day, great for adults and children alike. Leigh-Ann had spent the last couple of hours whingeing, but this completely captivated her and we all sat entranced, never wanting it to end.

It was (rather loosely!) based on a story of the Doctor and Zoe travelling in the TARDIS. The places they arrived at provided an excuse for the different acts – the Paddy Paine dancers singing and dancing enthusiastically – although a few of them did look like they were wondering what the hell they were doing at a Doctor Who convention, of all places!

I felt the format worked very well though and there was plenty of genuine talent on the stage from both the professionals and the amateurs. Wendy, Colin and Debs produced many of the magic moments of the day here, especially seeing Colin in his Sixth Doctor costume again. The script was clever and included Wendy reading her 'autobiography' with its many witticisms and puns. We had Colin in drag (He just can't resist!), then he paired up with Wendy to sing We're A Couple of Swells, both dressed up as tramps.

Debbie Watling repeated her star cabaret turn from the previous year, once again strutting her stuff in a high-cut sparkly black leotard. (Calm down, boys!) This time though, she added Cabaret to her repertoire as well as the hugely popular Big Spender.

After the show had finished, there was just time to get a couple more autographs from Wendy and to say goodbye to everyone. Our friends Pierre and Louis got kisses from Debs, while Leigh-Ann and I got kisses from Colin, so we all went home happy!

The convention as a whole was a very laid-back, pressure-free and relaxed affair. At the time, it was the only one I hadn't needed headache tablets for! The entertainment value was the highest of any conventions I had been to, with the stage cabaret aspect becoming more prominent each year. With quite a few conventions to choose from, I felt Ian Burgess had it exactly right and hoped he would continue in this vein.

The rest of 1999 was rather quiet with just a one day event brightening up our September. It was another Timeless one, this time presenting A Day in the Life of Nicola Bryant. It was held at Cardiff University and consisted of an interview, question and answer session, autographs, photos and a charity raffle.

Chapter Five
Millennium Rites

So, the 1990s were over and the 2000s had begun. Doctor Who and its stars had some good television exposure that year. The classic series had a short season of repeats on BBC2 at the start of the year, including The Silurians in January. It was good to discover it still had the power to scare children, as my daughter Emilia (aged six) had to watch it cuddled up to Nik! (She was a bit of a wimp though. She cried at Mulan!)

Genesis of the Daleks was shown in February. My diary entry for the 1st begins "It's 6:05pm and I'm just watching Doctor Who on TV! Gosh, it's good to say that!"

Peter Davison's new six-part series At Home with the Braithwaites began too. He appeared on This Morning with Amanda Redman on January 19th and the first episode was shown the following day at 9pm. It was an excellent series; I watched each episode and really enjoyed it.

Meanwhile, Sylvester McCoy appeared on See It Saw It as a spoon-playing granny! (What else?!)

Colin Baker was touring with the play Out of Order and we planned to see it when it came to Bath. I always know when it's been a while since I've seen Colin, as he pops into my dreams as if to remind me! This happened in February 2000, leading me to find out when the play would be coming near us.

Tom Baker was in the new series of Randall and Hopkirk (Deceased) which came out in 2000. Vic Reeves and Bob Mortimer played the title roles with Emilia Fox as Jeannie and Tom playing the God-like Professor Wyvern. It was a great series and Tom was impressive in his role too.

Following the first episode of Randall and Hopkirk

(Deceased), there was a This Is Your Life special, featuring Tom Baker! This was a wonderful programme. Tom is always brilliantly eccentric and this time, we could also spot people we knew there. John Nathan-Turner, Gary Downie, John Leeson and Lis Sladen all appeared on the show, as well as others we hadn't met such as Barry Letts and even Carry On star Richard O'Callaghan. (I'm a big fan of the Carry On films too.) It was very well done and Tom behaved himself, even though it was shown in a later time slot.

I continued my correspondence with Anthony Ainley and he was an excellent penpal, sometimes replying just a couple of days after I had sent my letter!

Our first Doctor Who event of the year was with The Master himself too, as we travelled up to Sheffield for An Afternoon with the Master organised by The Watchers. It was held at Sheffield Hallam University from 10:30am (despite its title!) until 4pm though we left around 3pm, as we were driving back to Bristol.

It was a long day for us and we spent six hours in the car for just five hours at the event, but it was worth it to see Anthony Ainley again and all three of us – me, Nik and Leigh-Ann – had a good time.

It was the usual format – interview, question and answer session, then the autograph queue. Anthony was very entertaining and witty, although as usual, he didn't reveal much about himself. He even told everyone there that he likes the fact fans don't know a lot about him! He did say he had never been married or had children, but didn't elaborate on the next obvious question that threw up!

Leigh-Ann asked a question and he told her she was 'gorgeous' and 'beautiful' and looked like a film star. When we met him, he was very friendly, charming and made time to talk to everyone. He even provided Murray mints and grapes for people to eat in the queue! We got quite a few different things signed as it was a generous limit of four free autographs per person. Leigh-Ann got a nice one that just said "Love from Anthony x'

He knew who I was when I told him my name and he appreciated how far we had travelled to see him. There were about five people there who had received letters from him and he said some of them had probably listened to his answer phone message. This intrigued me and I thought one day I might try to ring him too, just to hear what the message said!

In fact, it was just two days later – April 10th – when curiosity demanded I rang Anthony to hear this mysterious answer phone message. He had put his telephone number on top of the letters, so I rang him. The answer phone clicked in and a recorded message from 'The Master' began playing. I had planned to leave a message saying how much I had enjoyed meeting him again, but just after I said my name – he picked up! Eek! I hadn't planned for that. He said he screened his calls and only spoke to those he wanted to talk to.

It was amazing! I was nervous but we had a really good chat and got on very well, as we were talking for 23 minutes. We covered a wide range of subjects, including the Carry On films as it turned out he was also a fan of Kenneth Williams and owned his Audience With video and a copy of The Kenneth Williams Diaries. We also had a bit of a bitch about Barbara Windsor as I had met her as a child and she had been quite rude to me. He also said he had once gone through a gambling phase and had stood next to Sid James, who he described as "small, but very well dressed."

We talked about the event in Sheffield and he said he had been nervous and how he had been stopped by the police just before! I told him about being vegetarian and he said he was mainly veggie too.

He said he might go and do a bit of gardening and

explained that the area of London he lived in (The Hyde, NW9) was a nice area with lots of parks and gardens.

He spoke to Leigh-Ann too and asked her which football team she supported. When she said Manchester United, he told her he'd be watching their match on Sky that evening and hoping they would do well.

It was a brilliant experience talking to him and one I will never forget.

Nik and I went to the Theatre Royal, Bath on May 3rd to see Out of Order, the very funny Ray Cooney farce which starred Colin Baker and Deborah Watling as well as Gorden Kaye, Trevor Bannister and Henry McGee. We had a really good night and ended up in the pub with Debs Watling for an hour!

At the end of the performance, Colin noticed us when the cast came to the front of the stage to bow. We were sat in the middle of the front row of the stalls (our favourite spot) and Colin grinned and winked at us. Then we waited at the stage door to see him. He was commuting to High Wycombe so couldn't stay too long, but he was very sweet and friendly and explained he would have stayed if he could.

So we went to the pub with Deborah and had two glasses of white wine with her. (We bought one, she bought the other.) We chatted about conventions, the price of theatre tickets, other fans, my family and so on. She introduced us to some of the cast and it really felt like we were friends, not just fans. It was a lovely evening!

Nik and I were planning to go to the Weston-super-Mare convention coming up in July, but we discovered in May that it had been cancelled. We thought we would see if we could save up to go to Panopticon again, which was in Manchester in September - but in the end, we didn't do that either.

August 6th brought the annual Doctor Who Day at

Longleat. It was a real family occasion for us - Nik and I took all four kids (Leigh-Ann was almost ten years old, Dominyk was 8, Emilia 7 and Viktoria was 4) plus his parents, Glynis and Terry, went with us too. This meant they could keep the little ones amused with the attractions at Longleat while we queued with the older ones,

We got there around 11am and stayed until 5pm. It was a lovely day and we got to see a lot of people we knew from other conventions including Trevor, Ben and Ian Burgess. The celebrities at this one were Tom Baker, Deborah Watling, Nicholas Courtney plus John Nathan-Turner and Gary Downie. It was only Tom that didn't know us by then!

All of us met Tom and got things signed. Leigh-Ann, Dom and Emilia met Debs and Nick with us, but Viki was off elsewhere with her grandparents at the time. We gave Debbie some flowers and she remembered my name. Nick recognised us too. They were signing in the courtyard, while Tom signed in the Orangery.

Everyone was very friendly and Tom was in a jovial mood. Dom asked him to sign the tag of my Batty beanie and he did, he also tickled its tummy, ha ha! Viki asked Tom where to get a drink from and when I said that wasn't his job, he saved the universe; he thought that was really funny!

We first got Digital TV installed in October 2000. This gave us access to the Doctor Who that was shown on UK Gold 2. The stories we watched included Day of the Daleks and The Daemons in October, then The Sea Devils, The Time Monster and The Three Doctors in November. The year ended with Carnival of Monsters and The Time Warrior.

It was good to be able to all sit down as a family and watch Doctor Who on the telly, just like I did with my parents in the 1970s and 1980s! When The Mutants was on though, only Nik and the kids watched that. I chose upstairs on the Internet and watched Coronation Street instead! The stories were shown as an omnibus so that meant two or three hours of Doctor Who at a time.

The latter part of 2000 was difficult for us financially and we didn't have the money to go out much. This meant we couldn't go to any more conventions, but we did manage to attend three Doctor Who events in 2001.

Chapter Six
2001 - The Year the World Changed

We were lucky to have a local convention in 2001, as Blue Box IV took place at the Aztec Hotel in Bristol. It was over the Bank Holiday weekend in mid-April and included a half day's Doctor Who-themed Treasure Hunt, which is my strongest memory of the whole event!

We went in the car as it was the kind of treasure hunt where you have to go miles between each clue! In fact, it was even further than we had expected, as we visited at least four counties and cost us a bit in petrol and in the items we needed to buy along the way. I remember we had to obtain some gardening gloves from some farm, I'm not sure what else.

We went to some great Doctor Who locations though including the Rollright Stones used in The Stones of Blood, Oldbury Nuclear Power Station (The Hand of Fear) and the villages of East Hagbourne (The Android Invasion) and Aldbourne (The Daemons).

I think Oldbury Power Station was our first stop. Being in South Gloucestershire, it was right near us anyway and I had been round it previously when I was helping on a school trip. We didn't go inside it on this occasion though; I think the clue was at the reception.

The Rollright Stones were beautiful. They straddle Oxfordshire and Warwickshire and consist of several different areas of the stones. The ones I recall visiting on the treasure hunt were the King's Men, which is a fairly large circle of the stones and they are all spaced out and different sizes.

East Hagbourne was in Oxfordshire. I don't recall much

of it, except there was a church, a pub (the Fleur-de-Lys) and the Upper Cross (the stone pillar Tom Baker's Doctor was tied to in the story). It was here we stumbled upon Jason Thomas and some of the other Doctor Who fans also on the treasure hunt.

Our final destination was Aldbourne in Wiltshire. I had been hoping to meet some of the stars along the route and had been disappointed not to. However, Andrew Beech had taken some in his car and had done the course at a fast pace, so by the time we got to Aldbourne, they were all sat in the pub!

It is a beautiful village though and a lot of it is still recognisable from The Daemons. We saw the church (the Parish Church of St. Michael) and walked round the graveyard, where we met an elderly man working there who was around during the Doctor Who filming and could remember it going on. We also saw the village green and of course the pub.

The more recognisable aspect of a Doctor Who convention took place on the Sunday and Monday (15th and 16th April) when events were firmly rooted indoors in the Aztec Hotel. The special guests were three doctors - Colin Baker, Peter Davison and Sylvester McCoy, eight companions - Wendy Padbury, Deborah Watling, Anneke Wills, Mary Tamm, Mark Strickson, Sarah Sutton, Sophie Aldred and Carole Ann Ford (Louise Jameson had been due to go as well, but couldn't attend) plus UNIT's John Levene and visual effects genius Mike Tucker.

The interviews were held in the Cotswold Suite, the autographs in the Cotswold Foyer and the photo studio (which we didn't bother with again) was in the Mendip Room. Events began at 10am and finished around 6pm, though there was a celebrity karaoke on the Sunday night hosted by John Levene, though we didn't go to that.

I don't remember too much detail about this event at all.

I know we made a point of meeting John Levene and I bought a lovely 10x8 black and white photo from him which he signed. I did like him, but also felt he was slightly too Hollywood. Working in the States for a long time seems to give you a slightly enlarged ego, I feel and his personality just came across as a bit too big and a bit false.

I still didn't like Mary Tamm at this stage and never warmed to Carole Ann Ford much. She was always pleasant enough, but I just never seemed to 'connect' with her at all.

One person I do connect with is Anneke Wills and Blue Box IV was the first time I met her. She was fascinating to listen to at the convention and I remember chatting to her informally afterwards and thinking what an amazing woman she was. She was very unmaterialistic, spiritual and deep-thinking. Although I didn't agree with everything she said, I could really feel she was genuine. Whilst talking to you, she gives you her full attention and is incredibly charismatic and honest. Most people who meet Anneke seem to fall a little in love with her.

Sophie Aldred had her son, Adam, with her at this event, who was around a year old. At one point, she was sat on the low stage and he kept toddling off, trying to escape! He was a cute little boy and she shone in her new role as a mother.

Wendy Padbury was returning to the convention circuit after an eighteen-month break. One funny incident was when she was checking out of the hotel. She was writing the cheque out and as she signed it, she put 'Wendy Padbury x' and had to re-do it, explaining she had signed so many autographs, she hadn't quite managed to get back into 'business mode' and omit the kiss!

It was a fun weekend anyway and good to have a Doctor Who event pretty much on our doorstep for once!

Our next event was quite local, as we went to Longleat in August for its annual Doctor Who Day. Once again, we used it as a family trip out and this time the stars present were Colin Baker, Anneke Wills and Frazer Hines, along with John Nathan-Turner and Gary Downie, who organised it. There were also assorted monsters present – Cybermen, Daleks and the like, as well as Andrew Beech in costume as a Time Lord!

It was lovely to see Anneke again and I gave her a scented candle and some biscuits at this event. I received a lovely postcard from her a few days later thanking me for the gifts and commenting she had eaten all the biscuits in one go! She also said she hoped to see me again soon and she did, as we met her again at our next event.

Resurrection was a Doctor Who convention in Stoke-on-Trent, organised by Vortex Events and held in the Moat House hotel. This took place just four days after the terrorist attacks of September 11th and we hadn't really been feeling in the right frame of mind to go, but eventually had decided to. I became quite depressed following the news coverage and we decided it would be a good idea to get away from things for a while and enjoy ourselves.

The event was slightly muted and I think everyone who was interviewed on stage mentioned 9-11 at some point. I certainly recall Colin Baker and Paul Darrow making some kind of comment which was quite moving. It felt like we were all in this together, not letting the terrorists spoil our lives and all that, so there was a good 'community spirit' at this convention.

There were two Doctors at this one - Colin Baker and Sylvester McCoy, four companions - Sophie Aldred, Anneke Wills, Deborah Watling and Nicola Bryant, plus Barry Letts, Nicholas Courtney and Paul Darrow.

India Fisher was also there, although I don't think I was too bothered about seeing her, as I don't really 'do' audios. Nik loves the Doctor Who audio adventures though and is quite an admirer of India, so he went off to get a photo and a couple of CDs signed, while I did something else.

It was set out in the same way as conventions in hotels usually are, with the interviews being held in the main room (the ballroom at the Moat House), autograph sessions taking place in another large room (this time the Ballroom Foyer) then the photo studio was in the Brindley Room. It was again Robin Prichard and he still charged £12 to be photographed with one of the stars, £15 for two.

The autograph policy was slightly different at this event. We had badges with numbers on and you were called to get autographs in batches, depending on when your number was called. While this was basically a good idea, it did mean you sometimes had to make a choice between watching a talk or going to get autographs – but that isn't much different to other events really. Everyone has to choose between the two at some point!

The convention began at 10am on the Saturday and the first guest interviewed on stage was Anneke Wills, while Nick Courtney and Barry Letts began signing. This was the first time I had met Barry Letts and I found him to be quiet and rather serious, intelligent and polite. I liked him, but failed to find any great charisma. I think he was very thoughtful and deep and the sort of man you would get to know much better if you could have a one-to-one conversation with.

This was also my first time for meeting Paul Darrow. I had heard plenty of stories from Colin Baker about filming Timelash with him and didn't know quite what to expect. But Paul was amazing! His talk on stage was the highlight of the whole weekend and his talents as a raconteur is right up there with Colin himself, Tom Baker and Brian Blessed!

Paul Darrow was destined to be another of my 'crushes' as he was incredibly charming when I met him and of course, he's got that wonderful deep voice too. Poor Nik had to cope with me going on about yet another actor for a few months! He was very good though and even bought me a Paul Darrow calendar for Christmas that year!

The Saturday evening finished at 5pm after a panel with Big Finish Productions (again more interesting to Nik than me). In the evening, a screening of BBV (Bill Baggs' company)'s Have You Got a Licence to Save This Planet? was scheduled, but as neither Nik nor I can remember it, I'm not sure if it did.

The entertainment continued with two stand-up comedians (Andy White and Dave Donsdale) then singing from Jo Castleton, followed by a disco. Nik and I didn't stay in the Moat House hotel itself (I think it was either too expensive or fully booked by the time we got our convention tickets) so we don't think we saw the cabaret, but went to our own hotel instead.

I did meet Jo Castleton though and got a signed photo

from few of the spin-off films, including two of the Auton videos from the Bill Baggs and Nicholas Briggs team.

The Sunday followed the usual format with Sophie Aldred taking to the stage at 10am, while Sylvester McCoy and Nicola Bryant signed in the Ballroom Foyer. The day ended at around 5pm after Nicola Bryant's panel.

Overall it was another enjoyable convention and we were pleased we had decided to go after all.

For a long time, Nik had been urging me to watch Blake's 7 with him, as he was a big fan and owned the whole set of videos. I vaguely remembered it from childhood, but hadn't got much beyond seeing Colin Baker's guest appearance in one episode. (He played Bayban in City at the Edge of the World in 1980 and looks very sexy, strutting round in black leather gear!)

Well, now I had met Paul Darrow, I realised there was an attraction to watching the series after all! So Nik and I began to sit down in the evenings to watch the videos in order and it soon became one of my favourite programmes as well.

The year started and ended with letters from Anthony Ainley. In January 2001, he thanked me for my letter and Christmas card, wishing us all "a super duper '01" and hoping my little sister Beth (born in September 2000) would have "a super duper life". Referring to the recent flooding that some areas had been suffering from, he also wrote that he hoped we were "all high above any of those swollen rivers."

The one I received in December wished us "a lovely Christmas holiday and may '02 be especially good to all of you." He said he would hopefully be attending a convention in Bristol in the autumn and hoped to see us there. He signed the letter "A. A." drawing little smiley faces inside the 'A's.

Chapter Seven
Love and Loss - and Llangollen

John Nathan-Turner died on May 1st, 2002. Nik read the news on Teletext and told me. He died of liver failure and was only 54. According to the Doctor Who newsgroup (rec.arts.drwho), he had attended a recent convention in a wheelchair and had been waiting for a liver transplant.

It was a shock to me and I found it upsetting. I hadn't had to deal with much bereavement over the years and I was very sad. I felt I had come to know John quite well after spending three Llangollen weekends with him and I had a lot of respect for him.

I left a tribute on the Talking Point section of the BBC News website, which said -

"We met JNT several times at the Llangollen weekends and at conventions. He was a lovely man, very warm, witty and always fascinating to listen to. It was such a shock to hear he had died. He was the sort of man you always expected to be there. Things won't quite be the same, now he isn't."

I met JNT in March 1997, which was the first of several meetings over the years. The last time I saw him was in August 2001. I appreciated the fact he attended many conventions and was always happy to chat to fans and personally reply to letters.

He was a controversial figure and some fans never forgave him for his decisions while producing Doctor Who – Colin Baker's gaudy Sixth Doctor costume or casting Bonnie Langford as a companion were particularly unpopular. But he was a great spokesman for the programme and never ceased to love and promote the show in all its forms.

He was well-spoken and intelligent, openly gay, a witty raconteur, a charming and eloquent man, a warm and friendly one too. He was full of fascinating stories about his time working on the programme too and I had recently enjoyed reading his Memoirs, which had been published in Doctor Who Magazine.

Of course he wasn't perfect. He liked a drink or two (or three!), he smoked, and he had a biting wit if annoyed. But my memories of him are full of warmth and affection.

I will always remember JNT singing karaoke until the early hours. He was often the first to volunteer, performing a mean solo of Fly Me to the Moon and leading a whole bunch of us in My Way and Daydream Believer. These songs will always remind me of him.

John Nathan-Turner was so full of life, that he was one of those people you somehow don't expect to die. You just assumed he'd always be there.

By this time, Nik and the kids had got into a routine of watching Doctor Who videos on a Sunday evening. (I sometimes joined them, but often used it as a time to catch up on housework or nip onto the Internet!) They started with Jon Pertwee's stories and moved through the series (and Doctors) in order.

Leigh-Ann was now 11, Dom was 10, Emilia was 9 and Viki was 6 years old. We could gauge the success of a story by how long they all stayed for. Something dull would mean the kids would wander off when they got bored, leaving Nik to watch it by himself. A brilliant story would mean all of them would be riveted to the television for a couple of hours.

Nik and I would often try to guess how successful a particular story would be in holding their attention. We had a few surprises though. We had expected Four to

Doomsday to be a real low point, but instead Dom surprised us by not only sitting through the entire story, but really enjoying it too!

Nik and I got married on July 25th, 2002 – exactly five years to the day since we had met at Llangollen on the treasure hunt. After the ceremony in Bristol, we drove to Llangollen for our honeymoon and even stayed in the same hotel we had been in for a couple of the Travellers in Time weekends.

We had a lovely time and it was great to return to this special place. We went round the Doctor Who Experience for what would turn out to be our final time. It had opened in 1996 but closed for good in 2003.

The exhibition was very special and held lots of memories for us. Going round it with Nik was enjoyable, but it was tinged with sadness thinking of the times we'd been shown round it by John Nathan-Turner. It was quite a poignant experience.

There was a reconstructed 1960s living room with a small television playing the first episode of the programme. There were several displays of Daleks, including one which was half a model so you could sit in it and make the 'Exterminate!' sounds through a voice modulator, while watching your Dalek in a large mirror.

There were lots of Cybermen too including heads of all the different versions and full-size models in a cabinet. There was the Melkur in another cabinet which we were told had to be reduced in size before it had fitted into the display. There were also Vervoids, which Colin Baker had posed with during one of the weekends and a big hairy Yeti which Wendy Padbury had been photographed with, happy to cuddle into it until she was informed it had fleas!

Lady Peinforte's statue from Silver Nemesis was housed at the exhibition too. If you photographed it a certain way, it looked like it was glowing – very effective. K9 was always a good attraction and I also liked Fifi, the dog from The Happiness Patrol. The Malus from The Awakening was another excellent item.

The exhibition housed a wide range of costumes too, including those worn by the Doctors, companions and the Master. Adric's pyjamas were there, the Fifth Doctor's cricketing costume and the Sixth Doctor's multi-coloured ensemble alongside the elegant robes of the Time Lords. Display cabinets also housed an impressive collection of props and accessories used throughout the time the programme was being made.

One of the video presentations was a continuous loop of the Doctor's regenerations. This was in a quiet corridor and I remember watching this through several times in 1997, as it was the first time I had seen all of them.

It was a wonderful exhibition and it is so sad to think of Llangollen being without it.

The annual Doctor Who day at Longleat took place on August 4th with Sylvester McCoy and Sophie Aldred. We had been hoping to go, but couldn't afford it with the wedding costs and everything, as it was only ten days after we had got married.

By this time, I was regularly watching Nik's Blake's 7 videos with him and we had just finished viewing the second series. It was announced in August that Paul Darrow was going to be at the Avalon convention in October, along with Colin Baker and Anthony Ainley! Three of my favourite men all together! So I really wanted to go and planned to use my birthday money to pay for the tickets.

On August 26th, I watched and taped Hollyoaks as both Sylvester McCoy and Paul Darrow were on it. Sylvester played a character called Leonard Cave, while Paul was a judge – one of the roles he seems to play quite often, unsurprisingly perhaps given his presence and his powerful voice and gravitas.

Nik and I went to the Theatre Royal in Bath on August 29th to see Corpse! – a play by Gerald Moon which starred Colin Baker (as Major Ambrose Powell), Mark McGann (playing two roles – both Evelyn and Rupert Farrant), Louise Jameson (Mrs. McGee) and David Warwick (as Hawkins). The action of the play is based during December 1936 in London and takes place in just two sets – Evelyn's flat in Soho and Rupert's house in Regent's Park.

It was an excellent play and well worth seeing. It involved lots of costume changes and rushing around the set. Mark McGann in particular would disappear off the set one side, then reappear the other side in just a few minutes and dressed completely differently. Exhausting to perform, no doubt, but wonderful to watch.

The Theatre Royal in Bath is a great theatre with a lovely atmosphere. Stephanie Cole often watches plays there too and she was in the audience at this performance too.

As Colin took the last curtain call, he spotted us sitting on the front row and said something about seeing us out front afterwards. So we waited outside the stage door. Mark McGann came out first and signed my programme. He was lovely, very good looking and sweet.

Then Colin came out and chatted for a while, asking how the kids were and about our wedding. We had sent him an invitation, but he said he hadn't received it, though he had been on holiday in Cornwall anyway, so wouldn't have been able to attend. He autographed my programme 'Congrats you two! Love Colin Baker.'

Louise Jameson and David Warwick came out of the stage door together after this. David had played Kimus in The Pirate Planet in 1978 (and would be in the new series in Army of Ghosts in 2006) and is Louise's long-time partner. They happily signed my programme too and were both very friendly.

After that, Nik and I walked back from the theatre to the

car park. As we got near there, a car slowed, the window was wound down and Colin popped his head out, grinned at us and waved.

By the middle of September, we heard that the Avalon convention has been cancelled. This was a big disappointment. Although I did get to meet Colin again (several times!) and Paul Darrow, I never had another opportunity to meet Anthony Ainley.

My Dad got remarried on September 29th so we were all up in Lincoln. While we were there, I went to the Theatre Royal with my Mum to see Murdered to Death by Peter Gordon. This was a murder mystery spoof in the style of Agatha Christie. It starred Trevor Bannister, Nicholas Smith, Anna Karen, Richard Elis and Geoffrey Davies.

While Trevor Bannister and Nicholas Smith were both best known for their regular roles in Are You Being Served?, Nicholas also appeared in Doctor Who, playing Wells in The Dalek Invasion of Earth in 1964. Anna Karen was well known as Olive in On the Buses (and now as Aunt Sal in EastEnders), Richard Elis played Huw in EastEnders and Geoffrey Davies was a star of Doctor in the House and the subsequent Doctor series of the 1970s.

It was an excellent cast and the play was pretty good. I met some of the actors afterwards – Richard Elis was lovely, Trevor Bannister was nice enough, but seemed very old and Anna Karen was very sweet, chatty and down to earth.

We hadn't been to any conventions in 2002, but at least we had seen a couple of plays and returned to the Doctor Who Experience at Llangollen for a final time.

Chapter Eight
Changing Tactics

Over the years, our attendance of conventions had decreased a lot. From 1997 to 2001, I had attended 24 Doctor Who events. From 2002 to 2005, we only went to one and that was Longleat, which was more of a family day out than a fully-fledged convention.

The cost of going to conventions had escalated. As well as dealing with higher hotel prices and entry tickets, it was becoming more and more normal to charge for autographs, adding further to the spiralling costs for fans.

Some events were advertised then cancelled, while even the big names like Panopticon were struggling. They hosted Forty Years of a Time Lord in November 2003 and held it in the Hilton London Metropole. We had wanted to go, especially as Paul McGann was headlining and we hadn't met him. (We still haven't!) But the Hilton hotel prices were way out of our league and there was no way we could manage it. That was the last Panopticon convention.

As a family with four young children who all loved the programme too, it was impossible to afford for all of us to go. We instead shifted our focus to theatre trips for a few years. The children weren't usually so bothered about going to see a play so we only had to buy tickets for me and Nik and these were often around £20 each. Of course we also didn't need to worry about affording hotel stays or buying autographs or photos.

We managed to at least see Colin Baker in a play once a year in 2004, 2005, 2006 and 2007. Living in Bristol means we are in driving distance of many good theatres and if Colin didn't come to the Theatre Royal, Bath, we could usually get to see him in Cardiff, Malvern or Cheltenham.

The one event we did get to in 2003 was the final Doctor Who Day at Longleat and again, Colin was there, this time accompanied by Sophie Aldred and John Leeson. We made it a big family day trip again and as well as me, Nik, his parents and the kids, we also took our dog along this time! Yes, our Katy, the one who was named after Katy Manning. She was a wonderfully behaved dog, a Jack Russell cross Chihuahua and was much easier to entertain than the kids could be!

It was August and the sun was out again. I remember Colin looking very fetching in a straw hat. I think this was the event where I gave Sophie a parenting book. It was one on looking after sons that I had heard good things about – Raising Boys by Steve Biddulph. She'd probably had her second son by this time or was about to.

It was a fun day and it was great to meet Sophie and John again. As usual though, chatting to Colin was the highlight of the day for me. He had now met pretty much my whole family – my husband, my four children, my Dad, my mother-in-law and father-in-law and now our dog!

It was six months before we saw Colin again. He came to the Theatre Royal, Bath in HMS Pinafore and we went to see him on February 4th, 2004. One of the best things about going to watch Colin's theatre work over the years has been that we have ended up seeing all kinds of different productions, including some of the type we would not have seen otherwise. While Nik and I both love drama, comedy and farce, Colin was directly responsible for our first forays into horror, 18th century classics and – in this case – operetta!

Gilbert and Sullivan wrote HMS Pinafore and it is a comic opera which is thankfully quite easy to follow and has some great music in it. Amongst all the roles for established opera stars, the main acting role in this is the character of Sir Joseph Porter and this was the part Colin played. He did have to sing, of course, but carried it off beautifully with his comic timing and versatile acting. Nik and I had been unsure as to whether we would enjoy HMS Pinafore, but we really did.

The one convention we attended in 2004 was not a Doctor Who based one, but a Blake's 7 event called Star One. It was held at the Bedford Moat House, Bedford over the weekend of April 24th-25th and four of us stayed in the hotel as we took Dominyk (12) and Emilia (11) with us to this one. They had also been watching the Blake's 7 videos with us and had become fans.

The special guests were impressive at this one – Jacqueline Pearce, Gareth Thomas, Paul Darrow and his wife Janet Lees Price, Stephen Greif, Steven Pacey, David Jackson, Glyn Owen and Michael Keating. Doctor Who fans will be familiar with many of these names too, of course.

Four of them had appeared in Doctor Who on TV. Jacqueline Pearce was a memorable Chessene in The Two Doctors (1985), Paul Darrow appeared in two stories (The Silurians in 1970 and Timelash in 1985), Glyn Owen played Rohm-Dutt in The Power of Kroll (1978) and Michael Keating was Goudry in The Sun Makers (1977).

Two more of the actors would later be associated with Doctor Who in other media. Gareth Thomas was in the first Eighth Doctor Big Finish audio Storm Warning in 2001 and would later appear in an episode of Torchwood in 2006. Stephen Greif was a guest star in the Fifth Doctor audio drama Primeval in 2001 and later provided the voice of Gurney in Doctor Who: The Infinite Quest in 2007.

The event was organised in a similar way to the Doctor Who conventions we were used to, but in some ways, Star One was a bit more informal and we seem to have lots of access to the actors. I remember chatting to Gareth Thomas at the bar and Dom recalls the male actors smoking cigars together in the evening.

Steven Pacey was excellent with the kids, as was Jacqueline Pearce. Dom and Emilia kept going up to Steven in the evening and he was always good-natured and happy to chat. They felt Jacqueline was a bit of a soul-mate too and kept going back to see her while she was signing and she always gave them attention and a ready smile.

There were a few craft stalls in the hotel. Dom bought a skull ornament there, which he gave to Paul Darrow and I think we bought a little present for Jacqueline too. There was one stall selling pretend money with the faces of the Blake's 7 cast on and handmade designs on pillowcases. We later ordered a Servalan pillowcase from the woman who made them, buying it on eBay.

Nik recalls Paul Darrow and Steven Pacey being on stage together and delivering the best panel of the weekend. I liked both of them and felt they came across very well. I still had my crush on Paul, but rather liked Steven too. For once, we did pay to go to the photo studio. I had my photo taken with Paul and Steven, while the kids were photographed with Jacqueline Pearce.

Series 1 of Blake's 7 have just been released on DVD, so we got that signed by the cast. There were also small gatherings with around ten attendees per actor. These were little 'Coffee with…' extras and we had to pay for tickets for these events separately. I remember going to Stephen Greif's talk. He was an interesting man, but there was something slightly cold and intimidating about him.

I loved Gareth Thomas and although he seemed to spend an awful lot of time at the bar, he was very charismatic and entertaining. I also really warmed to David Jackson who was a wonderful character and a very friendly and lovable man. I was sad when he died the following year (July 25th, 2005), ten days after his 71st birthday. Glyn Owen also died a few months after the Star One convention on 10th September 2004.

The Doctor Who world lost one of its most special treasures in 2004 as Anthony Ainley died on May 3rd aged 71.

I remembered my first impressions of him from 1997. John Nathan-Turner and Gary Downie had told me Anthony was awkward, a difficult man and one who famously turned down personal appearances if the fee wasn't high enough.

Then I met him at Weston-super-Mare in 1997 and found him to be lovely and very gracious and charming. We corresponded for several years and his letters were friendly, witty and idiosyncratic.

We met him again at Sheffield. He remembered us, was very warm and extremely funny. He was a great raconteur, full of fascinating stories with just the slightest hint of indiscretion.

Then there was that telephone call I will never forget! We continued to write, then I suffered with depression and lost touch with everyone. Only in the first few months of 2004, I started feeling strong enough to write an occasional letter. I'd had writing to Anthony on my 'to do' list for a while, but didn't get round to it. I never thought there was any reason to hurry. Anthony was slim, fit and healthy and only in his 60s after all.

Then in May, I heard he had died and it was too late.

Someone online pointed out there was an obituary in The Independent. At first, it was seen as a rumour and there was quite a lot of hope that it was false. I kept refreshing Outpost Gallifrey and the BBC Doctor Who websites and eventually, the sad news was confirmed.

While I was on the computer, I was listening to LesMiserables on CD. As I first read the rumour (as it was then), I was listening to Michael Ball singing 'Empty Chairs

118

at Empty Tables'. By the time the rumour was becoming more concrete, the room was filled with Alun Armstrong crooning 'Master of the House'. How apt.

Anthony's life was very private and he never married, which seems to have made any definitive news hard to find. Apparently he was in hospital and died a few days after finishing his stay there. He had lied about his age and even the newspapers seemed unsure, but it looks likely he had been 71, not the 66 he had suggested.

It is sad when anyone you admire dies. It is even sadder if you knew them, if you had met them, written to them and cared so much about them. I really regret not writing that final letter. I hope he didn't think I had forgotten about him.

Anthony Ainley was a rare actor and a rare man. I miss him.

Chapter Nine
Enter the Ninth Doctor

2005 was an incredibly exciting year for Doctor Who as the series returned. It starred Christopher Eccleston with teenage pop star Billie Piper playing the companion Rose Tyler. The first episode, Rose, saw the return of the Autons and was broadcast on BBC One on 26th March 2005.

I had been very excited about New Who. I was one of those optimistic fans who always expected the programme to return at some point, but I was desperate for it to be great. The trailers were very eye-catching and the series itself didn't disappoint.

The only real concern I'd had was whether Billie Piper could actually act. I had firmly categorised her as a singer and not a great one at that, but it soon became obvious she was indeed a capable and talented actor and she was a wonderful companion.

Christopher Eccleston can always be relied upon to deliver and did a great job as the Ninth Doctor. I felt this series hit all the right targets, unlike the 1996 TV Movie. Doctor Who had to move on, it was a new era and the audience demanded more – faster paced episodes, better special effects and a kind of soap opera feel to it as we came to know Rose's family as well.

The TV Movie had tried to make it modern Who for a new generation of kids, but instead it had been too American and hadn't successfully targetted any demographic. It didn't hook the kids and the old established fans failed to recognise it as part of the long-running sci-fi series they knew and loved.

The 2005 series got everything right. This was largely due to the guidance of Russell T Davies who understands both the needs of the fans and the demands of the television industry. In the past year or two, some fans seem to have turned on RTD in JNT-like fashion, which is not at all helpful. His place in the building blocks of the new series must be recognised and applauded.

The first series had some wonderful episodes – The Unquiet Dead (the first time I became aware of Eve Myles), The Empty Child, The Doctor Dances and Robert Shearman's brilliant Dalek, which made me cry! The only episodes I didn't care much for were Aliens of London and World War Three. Farting green aliens were a bit juvenile for me, I'm afraid!

But overall, a great start. However, on March 30th – after just one episode - it was announced that Christopher was leaving, after completing only one series! I didn't know much about his replacement David Tennant at the time, but didn't like the look of him. However, we took the kids to the cinema to see Harry Potter and the Goblet of Fire and there was Mr. Tennant as Barty Crouch Junior and oh my, he's rather sexy! He could act too, which helps. The future for Who looked rosy after all…

Meanwhile, Nik and I decided it was time to see Colin Baker again. He was touring with Dracula in 2005. Being rather a wimp, Dracula is not something I would have gone to see usually, as I hated anything that could be classed as horror at the time. I really wasn't sure what to expect. I was only vaguely aware of the basic story of Dracula, having successfully avoided all the films and books about it, so I approached it with an open mind.

It was another trip to the Theatre Royal, Bath to see Bryony Lavery's adaptation of the classic Bram Stoker story of all things vampiric. Nik and I went one Wednesday evening in May and sat in our favourite seats - in the middle of the front row of the stalls. I like it there, as it feels like we are so close that we are really involved in what is happening on the stage. Also, if I am at the front, I can't see the audience behind me, which helps me with my agoraphobia!

The first thing we noticed was the striking set. It consisted of several levels with ramps and steps, all painted black. This was used for the different scenes and provided convenient areas to be used for separate rooms or locations. This also meant that Colin and the other cast members had to be very energetic, running up and down to various parts of the set. It also enabled the audience to be able to follow the action in several places at once.

In the front right of the stage was a computer and monitor and on the back of the set, there was a large screen. This is a good indication of the focus of this adaptation, as it was firmly set in the present day and used modern technology. The screen featured emails sent by the characters, photos they took on mobile phones, webpages accessed through the internet and so on.

Ben Keaton (Spencer in Casualty) was outstanding as Renfield, the asylum patient with a strange fascination for various creatures who seems to flit worryingly between clarity and insanity. Keaton displayed what an amazing actor he is, throwing himself completely and physically into the role. His performance remains one of the best I have ever seen on stage.

Colin Baker played the iconic part of Van Helsing with his usual authority and gravitas. His physical presence and the rich tones of his voice mean he is an actor that demands the attention of the audience and this was perfect for the role of Van Helsing, as the audience immediately feel he is trustworthy and will help those in danger.

In the performance we saw, Laura Howard was unable to play Mina and her role was taken by her understudy Eki Maria. Colin told us afterwards that Laura had perforated her ear drum shooting the gun on stage! Eki was amazing though, a real talent and you couldn't tell she hadn't been the first choice for the role.

I found it was more of a thriller than a horror overall. I

found I was edgy rather than scared - as proven by how high I jumped, when the gun shot went off! It was gory at times though and the special effects are very well done. Despite knowing blood capsules must have been used, I did wince at some of the apparent cuts and injuries.

Some of the effects were almost magic or illusions too and were very impressive. People seemed to disappear and one time was especially well done. This added to the overall feel of the piece and the enjoyment of the audience involved in it all.

At first, I found the play a bit strange. It was a bit complicated and confusing, but I soon got into it. It was very fast-moving and there were never any boring bits! It was a complex play and it is all to the credit of the cast and crew that they pulled it off.

We waited outside the stage door and met Colin again afterwards and had a conversation with him about what we thought to the play and general chit-chat.

Dracula remains one of the best plays I have seen Colin in. I thoroughly enjoyed it. It also helped to open my eyes to the wonders of the horror genre. I began to watch the old horror classics on DVD, including Bela Lugosi's Dracula and Boris Karloff's Frankenstein from 1931. While I'm still not a fan of modern horror, I love the Universal monsters and the films from the 1920s to 1970s. Another thing I have to thank Colin for!

2005 finished with the Doctor Who Christmas Day special and our first full adventure with David Tennant as the Tenth Doctor. The Christmas Invasion was good fun and the new Doctor was here to stay. Well, for a while longer than the Ninth anyway...

Chapter Ten
Tennant's Tenure, Theatre Trips and the Cavern

2006 began with some more sad news, as it was announced that Gary Downie had died on 19th January 2006 after a long battle with cancer. While I cannot honestly say this upset me in the same way as John Nathan-Turner and Anthony Ainley's deaths, it was a shame to think he was no longer around. While Gary had a sharp tongue and a venomous put-down, his exuberance and love for life lit up a room. Wherever he is now, I'm sure he's still dancing!

My Fair Lady came to the Bristol Hippodrome that month and I went to see it with my daughters Leigh-Ann (15) and Emilia (13). This starred Amy Nuttall (Chloe in Emmerdale), national treasure Russ Abbot (who would guest star in The Sarah Jane Adventures in 2008), Christopher Cazenove (best known for Dynasty), Stephen Moore (who I knew as Adrian Mole's Dad in the 1980s TV series, but recently earned his Doctor Who wings in 2010's episode Cold Blood), and veteran British actress Hannah Gordon (who Doctor Who fans may know as Kirsty McClaren in The Highlanders).

It was a very good cast, a high quality production and it also had great costumes and sets. We all enjoyed it and it was three hours long, so we felt we were getting our money's worth as it was quite expensive - £35 for an adult ticket and £30 per child.

We didn't stay to meet any of the cast afterwards, but while we were waiting for our lift, we saw Russ Abbot walk past, smoking a pipe and looking like an old man! It took me a while to recognise him and by then, he was across the zebra crossing and heading off.

Series Two of New Who began on April 15th 2006 with the Tenth Doctor and Rose continuing their adventures from the Christmas Special. My favourites from this were Tooth and Claw with its brilliant werewolf and horror homage, the exciting series finale and School Reunion. How wonderful it was to see Elisabeth Sladen back on television playing Sarah Jane Smith! Not to mention K9. Ah, my childhood had returned!

There were a few weaker stories I didn't enjoy so much though, especially the irritating Fear Her and I didn't understand the praise lavished on The Girl in the Fireplace either. Mind you, I was a tad biased as Sophia Myles was going out with David Tennant at the time and I admit to being rather biased against her for this reason.

David had completely won me over with his portrayal and I thought he was amazing. Along with millions of others, I fell in love and Tennant could do no wrong.

On April 30th, we went to our first proper Doctor Who convention for five years! It was Doctor Who @ The Cavern in Liverpool, organised by Erica Egerton. This time, four of us went as Nik and I took two of the kids - Dom (14) and Emilia (13).

The guests at this event were our old favourite Colin Baker, plus Deborah Watling, then three stars we hadn't previously met - Eric Potts (Diggory in Coronation Street, but also Oliver Charles in Aliens of London), Robert Shearman (the writer of 2005's Dalek) and Eugene Washington (who had played the scary Mr. Wagner in School Reunion).

We had an early start. We were up around 5:30am and left for Liverpool around an hour later on Sunday morning. The journey wasn't too bad and took us around four hours, but the early start and lack of breakfast meant that I arrived in Liverpool with a migraine with aura! I quickly took some

Migraleve tablets and thankfully felt well enough to go to the Doctor Who convention a bit later!

The convention was held at the famous Cavern Club, which is quite a grotty looking place really, several flights underground with low ceilings. Every time heavy traffic went overhead, the room seemed to shake, which was a bit unsettling at first!

The event followed the usual format with each guest being interviewed on stage and then there are opportunities to meet them, take photos and get autographs. However, because it was a smaller type of event and basically in one open-plan setting, this was a rare example of an event where the stage talks and the autograph sessions happened at different times. At the bigger conventions, both things happened at the same time and convention attendees have to choose between the two. This gave the Liverpool one a more relaxed feel, as we weren't trying to dash between two different locations.

There was also a charity auction, quiz and a few stalls of memorabilia to buy. The convention lasted about seven or eight hours.

All the guests were lovely and we all really enjoyed ourselves. As soon as Colin Baker saw us, he commented how far we had travelled from Bristol to see him! We told him it would only be another three weeks until we saw him again, as we had tickets to see him in Strangers on a Train in Cheltenham.

I got on well with Rob Shearman too, as we were talking about writing and I told him how much I had loved his episode Dalek and how it had made me cry. I said I had written 42,000 words of a novel, but had then hit a 'wall' and hadn't been able to write anymore. He was very interested and gave me his email address, telling me to make sure I kept in touch, which I thought was very kind of him!

Deborah Watling recognised us from previous

conventions, even though we hadn't seen her for a few years. She was looking a bit frail at this event and very tiny, so I was worried about her health.

Eric Potts brought his wife and kids with him and seemed to fit in really well with our big Doctor Who 'family'. Despite his part in Coronation Street being one of the most annoying TV characters ever, he was great in real life – witty, lots of fun and had plenty of interesting things to say.

Eugene Washington's enthusiasm for Doctor Who and his role in it shone through, both on stage and in person. He was great with Dom and Emilia too. When I asked him if I could photograph him with the kids, he struck a scary pose with his hands over their heads.

George Christopher was also there. He played Ziggy in Grange Hill and Jimmy Corkhill Junior in Brookside and as both Emilia and I love Grange Hill, we were thrilled to see him there. He was around the whole time, but as he wasn't an official guest star, he wasn't interviewed on stage and wasn't at the autograph sessions, as he has no connection with Doctor Who (besides being a fan!). He did conduct one of the interviews on stage though.

So I asked Erica if there was a chance Emilia and I could meet him, so we were taken into the green room and sat chatting on the sofa with him for about twenty minutes! This made two Grange Hill fans very happy! He was a lovely bloke, happy to tell us about his family and the attractions Liverpool had to offer.

Overall, the event was great fun, everything seemed to go smoothly and nothing seemed too rushed. My only complaint was that the stage was rather dark and this made it hard to take photos, but otherwise, everything was perfect.

While we were there, James Naughton recorded parts of the convention for his Doctor Who podcast (Podshock) and asked me and Emilia if we minded being interviewed for it.

We were happy(ish!) to go along with it and later on had the honour (and embarrassment) of listening to ourselves online!

Reviewing it now, I can't say I was thrilled with how I came across, but then I absolutely hate hearing my whiney voice on a recording! James began by asking if I was enjoying the event and I said I was, saying "I'm looking forward to meeting them next, that's the important thing." (My priorities have always been the same!)

I had already chatted to James before the interview, so he was well briefed about my convention experience, so once the tape was running, he commented that it wasn't my first convention and I agreed, saying I had been going to events since 1997. He also mentioned I had met my husband at an event in July of that year which James said was "really cool." Most things were 'cool' or 'awesome', incidentally. (Sometimes I feel so old!)

Next up, it was Emilia's turn to be tortured for public amusement – or as media types call it 'being interviewed'. He asked Emilia how long she had been a Doctor Who fan and she replied in a heavy Bristol accent - "Um, quite a long time, because most of my family are." (Yes, it's called brain-washing! Sit them in front of Spearhead in Space at four years old and don't let them move till they get to Survival!)

She was asked who her favourite Doctor was and she said it was Colin Baker. James said it was therefore 'cool' (obviously) that he was at the event that day, to which Emilia commented "Yeah. We've met him before, because my Mum meets him quite a lot." (She'd noticed my obsession then!) James asked her if she was enjoying the convention and she said "Yes, it's really fun listening to what they've got to say about it."

She was rewarded with Subway for dinner. There's nothing like a cheese salad baguette to shut up a thirteen-year-old girl.

Overall (and despite the embarrassment of the whole

interview thing!), the four of us had a brilliant day and it was great to get back into attending conventions again! We just hoped we could afford to make them more of a regular thing again in the near future.

It was back to the theatre as planned on May 24th as me, Nik and Leigh-Ann (by then aged 15) to see Strangers on a Train at the Everyman Theatre in Cheltenham. Besides Colin Baker, this also starred Will Thorp (who was in two episodes of Doctor Who in 2006), Alex Ferns (best known for his portrayal of wife beater Trevor in EastEnders), Leah Bracknell (lady-loving Zoe Tate in Emmerdale) and1960s singer and actress Anita Harris.

Strangers on a Train was based on the novel by Patricia Highsmith and adapted by Craig Warner. For me, it was even better than the Alfred Hitchcock movie! I thought it was excellent, one of the best plays I had seen and the cast were superb.

Alex Ferns was outstanding as Charles Bruno and delivered a mesmerising performance. Will Thorp was great as Guy Haines too. Colin Baker played the part of Arthur Gerard (the detective who works out 'whodunnit') with his characteristic professionalism and presence.

We met Colin afterwards, but he couldn't chat for long as he had to pick up his daughter. We did have a few minutes though. He had quite a few people waiting to see him, including some fans with Doctor Who items to sign.

We also met Alex Ferns and Will Thorp who were both rather shy (especially Alex) but friendly and they both signed our souvenir programme. Leigh-Ann told Will she was hoping to go to the same Drama School as he had been to (Bristol Old Vic Theatre School) and he said it was brilliant there.

Doctor Who had a new spin-off series in 2006, with

Torchwood hitting BBC Three on 22nd October 2006. This followed the character of Captain Jack Harkness (played by the ominpresent John Barrowman) who had already appeared in the main series of Doctor Who. Torchwood was billed as being Doctor Who past the watershed and initially revelled in its chance to bring sex and swearing to the melee of monsters and mayhem, before toning down somewhat for future series.

The Torchwood team comprised of four others alongside Captain Jack – Gwen the policewoman who gets embroiled into the Torchwood activities unwittingly (played by The Unquiet Dead actress Eve Myles), Doctor Owen Harper (Burn Gorman), pretty boy Ianto (Gareth David-Lloyd) and Toshiko Sato (played by Naoko Mori who was Doctor Sato in Aliens of London).

I loved Torchwood straight away and so did my elder teenaged children. (Our youngest, Viki, was ten and not allowed to watch it.) It was dark, pacy, exciting and had an added element of danger. Major characters could die – and did. Doctor Who allows you the safety net of knowing the Doctor won't die, he'll just regenerate. Torchwood pulled no punches and killed off one of the main Torchwood team, Suzie Costello, in the first episode!

I had got back into writing to Doctor Who stars again by this time and asking for signed photos. 2006 brought replies from Camille Coduri, Freema Agyeman (I got in early, writing to her as soon as I had heard she was going to be the new companion!), Helen Griffin (Mrs. Moore in the 2006 Cybermen two-parter), Claire Rushbrook (Ida Scott in The Satan Pit and The Impossible Planet) and Elisabeth Sladen.

I had written to Lis to tell her how much I had enjoyed seeing her reprise the role of Sarah Jane in School Reunion. She sent me a signed postcard back saying 'Of course I still remember you! The picture is still with me and still enjoyed.'

She was filming for the new Sarah Jane Adventures at the time.

I had kept in touch with Rob Shearman via email and we had exchanged a few thoughts on writing and so on. I had sent him a couple of photos I'd taken of him at Liverpool and there was one he especially liked. So when he needed an 'official portrait' for his author's credit in the 2007 Doctor Who Storybook, he asked if he could use my photo! Of course I said yes and it appeared on the back cover flap of the annual.

As a thank you, Rob sent me a free copy of the Storybook and got it autographed by Noel Clarke, Steven Moffat, Mark Gatiss and all the authors involved. I was very pleased and this encouraged me to pursue my hobby of photography as well, which has become an increasing passion of mine over the last few years.

The year ended with the Doctor Who Christmas Special – The Runaway Bride – with Catherine Tate joining David Tennant as the rather annoying Donna. I wasn't so keen on this episode, but it was good to have so much Who on TV, that I could be choosy!

Another spin-off spiralled onto British television on January 1st, 2007 when an hour-long special introduced The Sarah Jane Adventures. While Torchwood was aimed at the adult market, Sarah Jane was catering for the children and was shown on BBC 1 around 5pm. Its full series of ten episodes began in the September.

Elisabeth Sladen played the title role of course and was joined by Tommy Knight as her adopted son Luke, with Daniel Anthony and Yasmin Paige as their friends Clyde and Maria. It was very well made and did well in the ratings. It certainly hit its market in my house with my youngest two really enjoying it.

The latest series of Doctor Who began on March 31st

with David Tennant being joined by Freema Agyeman as Martha Jones. I thought she was very impressive and she remains my favourite New Who companion.

Saturday nights once more had come to mean an evening of great family entertainment. Similar to my childhood TV schedule of programmes like The Generation Game and Jim'll Fix It, the BBC was producing a good variety of output to please the family audience. At this point, the TV viewing in our house centred on Doctor Who, Any Dream Will Do (Andrew Lloyd Webber's search for a Joseph) and Casualty, not forgetting a quick hike over to BBC Three for Doctor Who Confidential.

The stories for this season of Who included some excellent ones. The Shakespeare Code appealed to me as I love Dean Lennox Kelly and thought he was perfect for the part of Shakespeare. I also enjoyed all the little in jokes about his plays and the clever use of the English language. Blink was also outstanding and the final six episodes of the series are all amongst my favourites. Human Nature and The Family of Blood tapped nicely into my fear of scarecrows and I thought Harry Lloyd was superb as the creepy Jeremy Baines.

I was thrilled to have the Master back as well. It was amazing to have Sir Derek Jacobi in the role initially and then regenerating into John Simm was genius! John was fantastic too and I couldn't think of any better casting for the part.

There were a couple of stories I didn't like though, particularly Gridlock (just dull, though the Macra were a nice surprise) and Daleks in Manhattan which could have worked, but didn't quite manage to. But overall, an impressive series.

I was so enamoured with Blink that I wrote to the three main actors in it - Finlay Robertson, Carey Mulligan and Lucy Gaskell – and I was very pleased to receive personally inscribed signed photos from all of them.

David Tennant was busy proving his versatility and getting plenty of work outside Doctor Who. He starred in Recovery which was shown on television in February. He played Alan, a man whose life is changed by a life-threatening head injury. This was a moving and convincing drama and a good contrast to Doctor Who – as was the Comic Relief sketch he appeared in!

Our first theatre trip for 2007 came on June 1st when Nik and I went to the Theatre Royal, Bath to see the Alan Ayckbourn play Bedroom Farce. It starred two Doctor Who regulars - Colin Baker and Louise Jameson - alongside Natalie Cassidy (Sonia in EastEnders), Beth Cordingly (PC Kerry Young in The Bill) and James Midgley (from Cutting It).

The play is set in three bedrooms and follows four couples – Ernest (Colin) and Delia (Louise), Malcolm (James Midgley) and Kate (Natalie Cassidy), Jan (Hannah Yelland) and Nick (Timothy Watson), Susannah (Beth Cordingly) and Trevor (Ben Porter). It was a really good play, very funny and clever.

Afterwards we waited for Colin outside the Stage Door and had a chat with him. I gave him a birthday card for the following week and a copy of my poetry book Petals of Pleasure… Petals of Pain… as I had included him as one of the people I had dedicated the book to. He was quite impressed to see his name amongst other stars like Nadia Comaneci and Helena Bonham-Carter, who I also admire, and he was very happy with the book.

I spoke to Louise Jameson too, chatting about her recent guest role in Doctors and she signed my theatre programme. I also met Natalie Cassidy, who was incredibly small at the time (it was just after her workout DVD and she was maybe a size 6) and quiet, and James Midgley who was very friendly and down to earth.

A good evening all around. A very entertaining play and

getting to meet the actors is always a bonus. Plus it's great to see Colin now and again… (Hee hee!)

We had the Eighth Doctor in our sights on Saturday 15th September, when Nik and I went to Colston Hall in Bristol. They were showing the 1929 silent film Pandora's Box starring Louise Brooks as part of the Bristol Silents event. It was a gala screening featuring a brand new orchestral score composed by Paul Lewis and performed live on stage by the Royal Ballet Sinfonia. Paul McGann introduced it, standing on the stage and delivering a short speech about the film's history and how it had come to be shown that evening.

It was a wonderful film, Louise Brooks was stunning and it ignited an interest in silent movies for me too. Nik and I sat in the front row and had a great view of Paul McGann, but sadly he left once he had introduced it, so we didn't get the opportunity to meet him.

David Tennant is another Doctor who has successfully eluded us to date. We went to London in October 2007 for the filming of the Radio 4 programme Chain Reaction. This was David Tennant interviewing veteran actor Richard Wilson. It was held at BBC Broadcasting House in Portland Place, London W1. This was my first trip to central London for some twenty years! I had a phobia of travelling to the capital, but the idea of seeing David in the flesh was enough to overcome my fears for a day at least.

We had a long queue around the side of the building, waiting to be let in. Thankfully there was a Starbuck's just along the street, so Nik would wait in the queue while I nipped across to get a couple of coffees to sustain us.

The interview itself was very good. We got a seat just a few rows from the front, so we could see well. David was great and handled it all professionally. One of the funniest bits was when there was a break and David was called to one side to discuss something with the producer.

This left Richard Wilson alone on stage for a few minutes. David had given him one of the model figures of his character Dr. Constantine (from The Empty Child and The Doctor Dances), so he was sat there fiddling with it. He looked at the audience and quipped "Well, I'll just sit here and play with myself then!"

Richard had signed a few autographs before going into the BBC building and posed for a photo with a young fan. David had been more rushed and just scrawled his autograph on one or two items before being ushered inside. Afterwards, we decided to try to wait for any autograph opportunities that might present themselves.

Sadly, there were far too many fans waiting, including a group of very vocal and enthusiastic young girl fans. After quite a long wait, maybe an hour or so, we heard a whisper there was a taxi waiting round one side for him. We walked round to see and he did come out, but he was hurried into the taxi and whisked away. It was a bit disappointing, but the screaming mob of girlie fans could have been dangerous.

The programme was eventually broadcast on 28th February 2008 at 6:30pm on BBC Radio 4. It was interesting to hear the final edit and it came across as very entertaining, but I much preferred being there in person to hear the uncut version.

2007 finished with the now annual tradition of the Doctor Who Christmas special. Voyage of the Damned was one of the better Christmas Day episodes and the inclusion of pop megastar Kylie Minogue was another attraction. It was an inventive twist on the old disaster movies I love and worked well on most levels, rounding off the year on a high.

Chapter Eleven
Comings and Goings

Series 2 of Torchwood began on 16th January 2008 and was broadcast on BBC 2 this time. This improved on the first series and had several episodes which were very emotional and poignant, such as To The Last Man.

Julian Bleach (an amazing Davros in Doctor Who later on in 2008) was incredibly creepy and spooky as The Ghostmaker in Out of the Rain. Torchwood offered a good mix of horror, thriller and drama with little comedic bits thrown in for light relief. Freema Agyeman popped up in three episodes, reprising her role as Martha Jones very effectively.

My favourite actor in the cast was Burn Gorman, but sadly he left at the end of this series. As did Naoko Mori as Toshiko, but I wasn't so bothered about her.

The fourth series of Doctor Who began on BBC One on 5 April 2008. This saw the return of comedy genius Catherine Tate as Donna, which I wasn't looking forward to, after finding The Runaway Bride rather sub-standard. Thankfully my questions were soon answered in the third episode, Planet of the Ood, where Catherine's sensitive portrayal had me crying along with her at the fate of the Ood.

Anyone still left with doubts over her ability to succeed as a straight actress should have been silenced by Turn Left, where again her performance was outstanding. Bernard Cribbins was also superb as her grandfather Wilfred Mott and amongst the guest stars, we had Georgia Moffett who played the Doctor's daughter while in real life both being the Doctor (Peter Davison)'s daughter and the Doctor (David Tennant)'s girlfriend! Confusing, huh?

Our first Doctor Who related theatre trip for 2008 was in April, when I went to the Theatre Royal, Bath with Nik and Leigh-Ann (then 16) to see Colin Baker in She Stoops to Conquer.

This added another dimension to our theatre-going experience, when we went to see him in it. The play was written by Oliver Goldsmith and was first performed in London in 1773. It is a period piece and a comedy, but is plenty more besides. I certainly don't think I've seen anything else quite like it in the thirty-odd years I've been going to the theatre.

The play is set in Warwickshire in 1773 and the country mansion of Mr and Mrs Hardcastle, played by Colin Baker and Liza Goddard, who were married to each other in real life in the 1970s. Liza also played Kari in the 1983 Doctor Who story Terminus.

The Hardcastle's daughter Kate (Dorothea Myer-Bennett) is to meet Charles Marlow (Matthew Douglas) – the son of Mr Hardcastle's friend – in the hope that they will develop a romantic attachment and get married. Marlow and his friend George Hastings (Matthew Burgess) arrive in the village at the local pub – the Three Pigeons Tavern – and ask for directions to the Hardcastle's place. But Tony Lumpkin (Mrs Hardcastle's son from her first marriage, played by Jonathan Broadbent) is at the pub and although he does indeed direct them to the right place, he mischievously tells them it is an inn and the innkeeper has delusions of being rich and important.

Arriving at the Hardcastle's house, the first of the 'comedy of errors' presents itself. Marlow treats the mansion as an inn and his prospective father-in-law as an innkeeper, leading Mr Hardcastle to decide Marlow would not be a suitable suitor for his daughter. But Kate meets a different kind of Marlow and is determined to learn more...

The plot itself sounds complicated, but watching it, it is

easy to follow and is very cleverly done and very funny. It is a fast-moving story too with lots of action, so we were never bored, even though the running time (including the interval) was almost three hours.

It was a beautifully staged play which seemed expensive and lavish. The set was very unusual, as it appeared the set had been placed on top of the usual stage so as to create new flooring which curved inward slightly in the middle. The costumes were stunning and looked just as if they'd come from a big BBC period drama on Sunday evenings. The women's dresses were especially beautiful, big creations with bustles and layers of fabric. While not being an expert in 18th century fashion, it certainly felt authentic to me and helped me get into the story easily.

In my opinion, all the cast were excellent. It is an energetic play with a lot going on and told in a language which – like Shakespeare or Chaucer – takes a few minutes to get into. It is because of the actors themselves that the meaning of their words is soon communicated to the audience and after a short time, we were able to understand it all well.

The two established actors of the piece were Colin Baker and Liza Goddard, of course, and both were wonderful in their parts. But the talent of the younger cast members shone through too.

I hadn't really been sure what to expect when we went to see She Stoops to Conquer, but I was extremely impressed by it. I loved the music, which really gave a period feel to it. The costumes, hair and make up added to the authenticity and made the language accessible and a few scenes in, I was relishing it like I do Shakespeare or Austen.

The cast were superb and the plot engaging, fascinating and regularly laugh-out-loud funny. We thoroughly enjoyed it and came out talking about it, discussing its merits. To complete a wonderful evening, we met Colin Baker again afterwards and had a chat with him. He is such a brilliant man, who always has time for you and is happy to discuss your views on the plays he is in. Needless to say, we told him we loved it.

Leigh-Ann and I meet Colin Baker in Bath

The same month, we saw John Barrowman in concert at Colston Hall, Bristol. Nik, Emilia, Viki and I had seats in Row B of the Stalls, so we had a great view. As you would expect, it was an entertaining evening - fun, camp and cheesy! He looked very smart in some gorgeous suits and sang very well. He also chatted to the crowd and his personality spilled out in that larger than life way.

He brought his Captain Jack 'Hero Coat' costume onto the stage and even modelled it for his Torchwood and Doctor Who fans, looking very dashing as ever. He also produced the Elvis type outfit he had worn on Dancing on Ice, the white trousers and the top with the red and blue stars. He chatted about being on the programme and it obviously still annoyed him that he had been voted off early.

Connie Fisher came on stage to sing a few numbers too, looking very elegant in a long black dress with diamond jewellery. She won How Do You Solve a Problem like Maria? in 2006, when John had been a judge on the show. She had completed her role on stage in The Sound of Music a couple of months earlier. She had a lovely voice and was a pleasure to watch.

All four of us enjoyed the concert and he got us clapping along. It was a good night out, but despite enjoying it, we haven't bothered to get tickets for his other concerts.

Afterwards, there were loads of fans waiting to see if they could meet him. He's a popular guy! It was obvious he wouldn't be able to sign for people too well in that kind of crowd, but instead of just speeding off in a car with tinted windows, he compromised by coming out standing up inside a car. It drove slowly, so he could wave to everyone and we could take some photos.

Our only convention of the year was on June 14th when Nik, Emilia (15) and I went to The Oncoming Storm. This was held in the Guildhall in Gloucester, which was a lovely setting, a pretty building with plenty of space, nicely sized rooms for the events and a café area to buy drinks and snacks from.

This had a good mix of guests from the Classic series and New Who. From the Classic series, we had a Doctor - Colin Baker, a companion - Louise Jameson plus Nicholas Courtney, as well as two guest stars I hadn't previously met - June Bland (Berger in Earthshock and Elizabeth Rawlinson in Battlefield) and Wendy Williams (Vira in Ark in Space).

They were joined by a selection of stars from the new series – Francois Pandolfo (Quintus in Fires of Pompeii), Ryan Sampson (Luke Rattigan in The Sontaran Stratagem and The Poison Sky, as well as playing Alex in the sitcom After You're Gone) and Albert Valentine (who was the

140

creepy child in The Empty Child and The Doctor Dances). Albert was accompanied by his mother who is Alison Bettles, better known to fans of a certain age (Me!) as Fay Lucas in Grange Hill.

There were also Danny Hargreaves (special effects expert who works on New Who, Torchwood and Sarah Jane) and Jill Curzon, who played the companion Louise in the 1966 film Daleks' Invasion Earth: 2150 AD (with Peter Cushing as the Doctor).

The Sarah Jane Adventures were represented here by two of its young stars - Tommy Knight (Luke) and Daniel Anthony (Clyde). John Pickard was also there as the Fifth Doctor's companion Thomas Brewster in the Big Finish audio CDs. We also recognised him from Hollyoaks, 2 Point 4 Children and Grange Hill.

Gary Cady (Mark of the Rani) and Rex Robinson (three Doctor Who stories) were scheduled to attend, but did not.

It was a good fun convention. Jason Thomas was there and this would have been the first time we met Tristan Maddocks and his young daughter Eleanor. They are from Brighton and lucky Eleanor seems to have been photographed with almost all of the stars from both the Classic series and New Who. Lucky girl!

The Oncoming Storm began at 10am and finished at 6pm. There were interviews taking place on the stage in the main hall, a photo studio and the usual autograph signings. The stars sat behind a long table in a lovely room and we fans queued up for each one we wanted to meet. We could have two personal items signed free of charge per actor, with any additional autographs costing £5 each. With Colin Baker, it was only one free autograph per attendee but he would sign any of his own photos free of charge if you bought them from him on the day.

There was a free souvenir programme for each attendee and this was well designed with a clear timetable and a double page for autographs.

The day began with Jill Curzon and June Bland on stage, but we went to the autograph signings to meet the Sarah Jane boys. They were a big attraction, as I think it was their first convention. Emilia was a big fan and really excited about meeting them. It had been their names that had persuaded her to come to Gloucester at all!

Tommy Knight had his mum with him as a chaperone, as he was only fifteen. (He's about three months older than Emilia). Despite Daniel Anthony playing a schoolboy in the series and looking young, he was in fact 20 at the time, being born in October 1987.

Both boys were very polite and friendly and seemed to be enjoying it all, though they looked surprised to discover how popular they were, as they tended to have the biggest queues throughout the day. They seemed to get on really well with each other too. They were always sat next to each other, chatting and joking away.

The next signing session was with Danny Hargreaves, Jill Curzon and June Bland. We saw Jill, but didn't get chance to meet her. I didn't mind too much though, as I'm not a huge fan of the films.

June Bland was pleasant and well-spoken. She was nicely dressed too with a very pretty scarf that I commented on. She signed our programmes for us and we had a few words.

Danny Hargreaves made a big impression on us. He was lovely, very easy to chat to and down to earth. I took a photo of him, which came out very well. I told him I enjoyed seeing him on Doctor Who Confidential. He seemed a bit embarrassed by his appearances on that. Being a behind the scenes guy, I got the feeling he wasn't too enthusiastic about being in front of the camera, but he was great meeting people and came across as genuine and friendly.

There were several monsters around the venue, actors hired to walk round in menacing costumes and providing photo opportunities for fans. I seem to remember little

142

Eleanor was rather frightened by the Clockwork monsters and I had to admit I found them pretty creepy too. There was also a big green Slitheen, a Ha'ath and an Ood (which Emilia posed with for a photo). There were also static models around including a K9 and a Dalek on stage.

While a common misconception is the idea that all Doctor Who fans attend conventions dressed as monsters, the truth is that a small minority use it as an excuse to dress up in similar attire to their favourite Doctor or companion, often taking lots of time and effort to recreate the right look. However, the majority, me included, just wear ordinary clothes. But as these events are fun-filled family days out, the organisers of conventions are offering more entertainment for the kids these days and having the monsters walking around creates a good atmosphere.

The photo studio at this one charged £10 per photo, whether there were one or two stars in it. This was quite a good deal and as they were developed on site, it meant the finished photographs were ready in an hour or so, so we could hopefully get them signed afterwards as well.

Emilia and I had our photo taken in the studio with Colin Baker (A legitimate excuse for me to get a cuddle from him!), then we went through to the stage to hear the end of the interview with Louise Jameson and Wendy Williams.

We met Nicholas Courtney again when he was doing his autograph session. He was in good form, looked well and was very sweet and friendly. I took a lovely photo of him and got some items signed. I was talking to him about wanting the Brigadier back in the new series, as quite a few fans were saying the same thing. We didn't know he'd just been filming The Sarah Jane Adventures! It was a shame Nick was too ill to film his part in The Wedding of Sarah Jane Smith in 2009, but at least he was in one story in 2008. He certainly seemed healthy here, thankfully.

Daniel Anthony and Tommy Knight were up on stage

next, so we listened to their interview. It was interesting and they were good fun.

This was followed by us catching up with Colin Baker at the signing. We got some autographs, including on our Timelash DVD cover. He signed the photo of me and Emilia with him too, inscribing it 'For Emilia and 'er mum!'

It was then back to the photo studio for Emilia to be photographed with her favourite guests - Tommy Knight and Daniel Anthony.

This signing session featured Louise Jameson, Wendy Williams, John Pickard and Albert Valentine. We didn't get round to meeting Louise as she had quite a queue and as I had already met her at previous events, we prioritised the stars we hadn't seen before.

Emilia and I met John Pickard. Emilia knew him from Hollyoaks, so was keen to meet him and there was no-one queuing for him at the time. Admittedly his part in the Doctor Who world was quite small, but he was a well-known actor with several big roles to his name. We were certainly happy to spend some time chatting with him and at least the lack of a queue meant there was no pressure to rush, so we popped over a couple of times to see him. He was a lovely bloke, very nice looking, easy going and easy to chat to. Emilia and I both had photos taken with him, which came out well.

We met Wendy Williams too, who was quiet, but nice enough. Then we met young Albert Valentine, who was only ten years old at the time. He handled it all very well and took time to sign his name carefully in autographs.

His mum Alison Bettles was sat back behind him, but I started talking to her, saying I remembered her as Fay Lucas and asking if she could sign the Grange Hill annual for me, which I had brought with me. She was very sweet, a bit shy maybe and very modest. She was born the same year as me, but she looks great and has aged very well. I took a pic of her with Albert and Nik took a photo of me with Alison.

(He was very happy to do this, as he quite fancied her when she was in Grange Hill!)

Then John Pickard and Albert Valentine were joined in the signing room by Francois Pandolfo and Ryan Sampson, so we met them too. Ryan was very tiny and incredibly slim. He was very camp too. I took a photo of him while he was sat there and he was happy to smile for the camera.

Francois Pandolfo was drop dead gorgeous! Me and Emilia both thought he was stunning and happily snuggled up to him to have our photos taken with him! As well as his looks, he came across as very friendly and charming too.

We just had time to pop back to see Tommy and Daniel in the final signing session and took a great pic of them together. Emilia got the photo of her with Tommy and Daniel signed by them both. Emilia and Tommy chatted and he was thrilled to discover she was his age, as he had thought she was at least 17. He signed the photo with 'loads of love' and lots of kisses!

There definitely seemed to be some chemistry there and afterwards Emilia asked me to pass her mobile number onto him, which I did. Not that she ever expected to hear anything, of course.

The convention itself had come to an end, but as it was a Saturday evening, there was a free showing of live Doctor Who on the big cinema screen. The three of us stayed for that and sat down to watch the episode that was Midnight, which was excellent, even better for being a cinematic experience!

Tommy and Daniel came in and sat behind us, up near the back. A few minutes later, Emilia got a text message on her phone and it was from Tommy! They texted back a couple of times then after the episode had finished and people began to leave, Emilia waited for Tommy and they had a hug.

In the car journey home, Emilia still continued to

exchange text messages with Tommy and they kept in touch for a while afterwards through MSN, Facebook and text messages. They haven't met up since The Oncoming Storm though and haven't been in touch much lately.

Our next brush with celebrity happened closer to home, as Nik and I went to a book signing with Russell T Davies and Benjamin Cook at Borders in Bristol. A Writer's Tale was released 25th September 2008 and we bought a copy for us and one for my Dad for Christmas (as he is still a big Doctor Who fan).

We got both books signed and Russell and Ben were wonderful, absolutely fantastic! Russell was great, full of fun, the sort of guy you just want to hug as he was so warm and lovable. His enthusiasm for the series always shines through when he talks or writes about Doctor Who. I gave him a copy of my poetry book as he was one of the inspiring people I had mentioned in my acknowledgements.

We really enjoyed meeting them and presumably they

enjoyed meeting us too, as I got name-checked in Russell's column in the following issue of Doctor Who Magazine! Wow!

The book was excellent too. Over the years, I have read probably hundreds of Doctor Who related books - biographies, autobiographies, novelisations and so on. But I can honestly say, The Writer's Tale is the best Doctor Who book I have ever read!

The project began as a series of emails between Russell and Ben and this format is the basis of The Writer's Tale. Ben wanted to find out more about the process of writing Doctor Who from the initial ideas through the casting process, script writing, filming and editing. This is the side few of us see. We sit there enjoying the final television programme, blissfully unaware of all the hours of toil behind each one. I certainly found the book revealing, enlightening, informative and compelling reading.

It took me quite a while to read the book, because I wanted to take everything in and savour it. Nik, however, breezed through the 512 pages in a weekend. He loved it too.

Despite some sad parts, the tone of the whole book is one of fun and humour and - like Russell T Davies himself - it's large, warm and big-hearted with oodles of affection for Doctor Who, its cast, crew and history.

A Writer's Tale – The Final Chapter was later released on 14th January 2010, which featured a new cover (Russell T Davies with David Tennant and John Simm) and was updated with an extra 300 more pages. This new version included the part from Doctor Who Magazine where we were mentioned. There it is on page 458 – 'Karen and her husband ('We got engaged at a convention, and our dog's named after Katy Manning')' – yep, that's us.

The Sarah Jane Adventures began its second season on

148

29th September 2008. There were twelve episodes this time and it was another high quality series. This was the series that Tommy Knight, Daniel Anthony and Nick Courtney had been filming when we met them at The Oncoming Storm earlier in the year.

During their interview in Gloucester, Tommy and Daniel (who were not allowed to give much away, of course) said they had been filming in the woods just before the convention and this turned out to be the first story of the season – The Last Sontaran.

Nicholas Courtney reprised his role of Brigadier, though he had by now been promoted to a Sir, giving him the full title of Brigadier Sir Alistair Gordon Lethbridge-Stewart. He was in the final two-parter of Series Two – Enemy of the Bane. The recurring villain Mrs Wormwood (Samantha Bond) appeared in this one too. Yasmin Paige (Maria Jackson) left in the fourth story of this series and was replaced by Anjli Mohindra as new girl Rani Chandra.

On October 24th, 2008 (the day after my 39th birthday), Nik and I went to the New Theatre, Cardiff to see Noises Off starring Colin Baker, Ben Hull, Maggie Steed, Jonathon Coy, Liza Sadovy (who went on to be in two episodes of The Sarah Jane Adventures in 2009) and Richard Hope (who was later to be in Doctor Who, appearing in Cold Blood and The Hungry Earth in 2010).

I didn't know anything much about the play before. I had heard of it and knew it was written by Michael Frayn, but otherwise, nothing. It was to be a night of surprises – the first one being the words on the stage curtain changing from 'Noises Off' to 'Nothing On'. I was intrigued…

Act One begins with a fairly standard theatre set – the inside of quite a nice house, two-storey with a staircase and several doors, a sofa, TV, big window and small table. We meet Dotty, the housekeeper of said house, who starts by answering the phone.

Soon, we realise this is a cast rehearsing for a play called Nothing On, which opens the following day. This act is fairly straight-forward. We meet the cast and begin to get to know them – both as their character's name and the part they are playing in the play.

This act is clever, witty, interesting and funny – but not hilarious. The whole play builds up well from the slight tittering of the first act to the hysterical guffawing of the third!

Act Two is the cleverest act in many ways. The set is reversed, so we now view the back of it. It is a month after the dress rehearsal of the first act and there are plenty of tensions between the cast. We find out about various affairs going on and who has feelings for whom and all the conflicts coming out.

As we see the cast performing Nothing On from a rear view, we are privy to the backstage chaos. This is an act full of physical comedy, especially an impressive array of intricate and fast-moving throwing of props. There is so much going on, that it is hard to know where to look!

The final act sees the set back the right way, as it was for the first act. This is a further two months later and by this time, most of the cast and crew are feuding, so they try to trip each other up (often quite literally), while still somehow performing the play.

This is performed at a great pace, ensuring the audience is never bored. By this time, I had tears streaming down my face with laughter and I was full of admiration for the actors and how brilliantly they coped with everything. It must be so hard to remember the script as well as all the running up and down stairs, through doors and windows, while dealing with various props.

Maggie Steed played Dotty Otley in the run we saw. Liza Sadovy was Belinda Blair, with Richard Hope as Frederick Fellowes. Ben Hull tackled the energetic and physical role of

Garry Lejeune, while Jonathan Coy played the stressed director Lloyd Dallas.

Colin Baker was hilarious as Selsdon Mowbray, a long established actor who is now an alcoholic, so the cast and crew have to watch him. He can be inclined to disappear and can't be trusted around bottles of whisky!

The cast were all brilliant in these most challenging of roles. Colin was excellent as the drunken old pro, the lovable but slightly irritating Selsdon. He emerged from the back of the stalls and from the moment he arrives, you can see he's in character, with the slightly-too-wide smile that suggests a tad too much booze and a touch of senility.

Besides watching Colin, our attention was soon drawn to Ben Hull, who had a very physical role and his energy was amazing. We met him afterwards and he had his fingers strapped up from an injury he had sustained from the play. (Colin had been injured too.)

After the play, we met the cast, got autographs from them and had photos taken with them. Everyone was really lovely. We had a nice chat with Colin the first night as well.

Nik and I enjoyed it so much that we came back the following evening and watched it all again! Sadly this time, we missed seeing Colin though Ben Hull asked the theatre staff if they knew where he was. It was a rainy night and they were all rushing off home for the weekend, so it was a bit harder to meet them then.

We had once again really enjoyed ourselves and were full of it when we got home, telling the kids what a funny play it was. So Leigh-Ann and Viki asked if they could see it too.

By now, it had finished its run in Cardiff but we found out it was coming to the Festival Theatre in Malvern. So on October 30th, the four of us went there to see it once more. Nik and I had seen the play three times in a week! It is definitely the kind of play that is so brilliant, so much fun and so hilarious, that you want all your friends and family to see it.

Both Leigh-Ann and Viki loved it too. Viki has Aspergers' Syndrome and rarely goes to the theatre. We explained to her about the set turning round, so she knew what to expect before we went and she thought it was wonderful!

2008 finished with the now traditional Doctor Who Christmas Special. This one was called The Next Doctor and starred David Morrissey and Dervla Kirwan alongside David Tennant. As usual, it was classy, fast-paced and lots of seasonal touches. The image of Cybermen in the snow was one of my favourites as I love both. We also had the debut of rather cute Cyber-dogs in this one. Officially they are called Cybershades but as that sounds like a cross between a Cyberman and a lampshade, I prefer my version.

The media, of course, relished the combination of the episode's title and the association of David Morrissey, oft tipped to become the Doctor at some point. Rumours abounded that David M would soon be announced as the replacement for David T, but no, they were wrong again. David T would be back for 2009.

Chapter Twelve
26? I Have Ties Older Than That!

The year began with the most exciting speculation – and revelation – ever, about who would be the Eleventh Doctor. To capture my enthusiasm, here are two of my diary entries for January…

January 2nd – "Another day at home, though this one was a bit more exciting as it was announced that the BBC are revealing who is the Eleventh Doctor tomorrow – YAY! I'm really excited and desperately hope it will be Paterson Joseph, though the forums are favouring unknowns – David someone and Matt Smith. Anyway, we'll find out on Doctor Who Confidential at 5:35pm tomorrow!"

January 3rd – "The new Doctor is MATT SMITH! Who? Plus, he's too young (26). Like someone said on Facebook, they have *ties* older than that! I'm disappointed it isn't going to be Paterson, but by the end of the night, I was kind of resigned to Matt and I think I will end up liking the guy, as he's pretty quirky. Bit of a shock casting though."

Nik and I had been practising how to pronounce Chiwetel Ejiofor's name beforehand, as we felt he had a good chance of getting the role – but it wasn't to be. I still think that either he or Paterson Joseph would be excellent in the part and surely it must be time to have a black actor as the Doctor?

It really didn't take me too long to warm to Matt Smith though. He came across as incredibly likeable in the interview he did with Doctor Who Confidential and the more I found out about him, the more I thought he was absolutely right for the role.

Once I read statements from Steven Moffat, about how they knew he was perfect for the role once they had seen his audition, I became ever more convinced. The Moff rarely gets these things wrong!

In February, we had an opportunity to see Matt Smith in action, as he was in a new series called Moses Jones. While the programme itself was pretty confusing and not a great favourite of mine, Matt was impressive.

In May, Nik and I watched Party Animals on DVD, which we had bought purely because Matt Smith was in it. It was originally televised on BBC 2 in 2007 and followed the lives of some of the people who worked in Parliament. Matt played Danny Foster, a researcher to a Home Office Junior Minister.

It was an excellent series, well worth watching, a very intelligent and interesting drama. Matt really stood out and I was becoming more and more excited about seeing him in the role of the Doctor. I was happy to try to silence any remaining critics out there too. Don't worry, he'll be fine, this guy is really talented and has that little something you need for the character of the Doctor.

We knew Matt would start filming Doctor Who in July, so we were all excited to discover more – what his outfit would look like and who the new companion would be.

In the meantime, Nik and I watched more DVDs, including The Monocled Mutineer starring Paul McGann and Takin' over the Asylum starring David Tennant. I had seen The Monocled Mutineer when it was originally broadcast on BBC1 in 1986, when I was sixteen years old. It was one of those series that always stayed in my mind as being something special and one which impressed and moved me in equal measure.

Paul McGann played Percy Toplis, who deserts from the British Army during World War One. His quick-thinking and charm lead him to pass himself off as an Officer for a while and you admire his cunning and audacity, yet all the time, he is getting closer to being caught. It's a fascinating series and a must see. This was the first time Nik had seen it (being only 11 years old in 1986!) and he really enjoyed it too.

I remember I had quite a crush on Paul McGann at the time and started collecting a few pictures of him. I never fancied him as the Eighth Doctor though, but many did. There seemed to be a feeling amongst some female Who fans in the late 1990s that McGann was the first fanciable Doctor ever. (Of course, I dispute that, finding the Sixth Doctor much sexier!)

Takin' over the Asylum was a six-part drama made by BBC Scotland in 1994, when David Tennant was in his early twenties. It is set around a hospital radio station in a psychiatric hospital. Ken Stott plays the DJ Eddie McKenna (brilliantly) and David is one of the patients, the manic-depressive Campbell. A wonderful piece of acting by him and a fantastic series all round.

Moving forwards to 2009, David Tennant had less Who to keep him occupied with a decision being made that instead of a full series, there would just be four Doctor Who Specials spread out across the year. Before the first one aired in Easter, he presented some of Comic Relief. He was very good. He did really well at the Mastermind section they had, when he was answering questions on Doctor Who. It's wonderful to know he was a fan of the series himself before! Memorably, he also snogged Davina McCall! Well, it's for charity after all and you do what you have to do…

The Doctor Who Easter Special was on TV on April 11th, so I watched it with Nik and Leigh-Ann. It was Planet of the Dead with Michelle Ryan as Lady Christina. My verdict? Okay, but nothing special. They showed a trailer for the next one though (The Waters of Mars) and that looked much better! I prefer the darker ones and the other three were supposed to become increasingly dark, as the series moved towards the regeneration.

In March, I went to London to see Oliver! at the Theatre Royal, Drury Lane, London with Leigh-Ann (by now 18) and my friend Jayne. Previously, my phobias of travelling and going to London had prevented me from going to something like this, but I really wanted to see Oliver! and it was my first time ever attending a West End show.

It had an amazing cast too - Rowan Atkinson (Curse of the Fatal Death), Jodie Prenger (the winner of the I'd Do Anything series to find a Nancy), Burn Gorman (Owen Harper from Torchwood), Julian Bleach (Torchwood and Davros in Doctor Who) and Julian Glover (who had been in Doctor Who twice – in The Crusade in 1965 and City of Death in 1979).

The show started at 7:30pm and when we arrived, there was a sign up saying that Jodie Prenger was ill, so Tamsin Carroll would be playing Nancy instead. This was disappointing, but we had our favourite Oliver in the role (Gwion Wyn Jones) plus Rowan, Burn and the two Julians, so I was happy enough!

The show was amazing and I absolutely loved it! Rowan Atkinson was perfect as Fagin, a truly fabulous performer! Afterwards, we waited by the Stage Door. We saw Julian Glover and Julian Bleach go past, but didn't stop them. (Julian Bleach looks so different in every role, we weren't quite sure what he looked like in real life!) Sadly we missed Burn Gorman, who I would have loved to have met. After an hour's wait, Rowan Atkinson came out and signed autographs for those waiting and posed for photos, so that made the wait worthwhile.

A Burn Gorman-less series of Torchwood was shown on BBC 1 in July. Instead of a complete season spread over weeks, Torchwood: Children of Earth was televised over five nights as a mini-series. It was an excellent series and Liz May Brice was a great addition to the cast, but the last episode left me feeling a bit empty and as though it was the end of Torchwood forever.

Nik and I had a weekend away in London in July. Now I had conquered my fears, a whole new world of London theatre had opened for me and I had great reason to go again. We had tickets to see Neil Pearson (one of my favourite actors) in the play Arcadia at the Duke of York theatre and we were also going to try to get tickets on the day for Ibsen's A Doll's House starring Christopher Eccleston. It was sold out, but they sell a few tickets on the day to first-comers.

This necessitated an early start. We got up around 5am (after about four hours' sleep!), caught the 6:30am train from Bristol Parkway and got into London Paddington around 8am. We got the Tube over to the Donmar Warehouse and queued for tickets there from around 9am until the doors opened at 10:30am. We weren't near enough to the front to get seats, but we did manage to get standing tickets and they were only £7.50 each!

We saw the 2:30pm performance of A Doll's House and the play lasted around 2 ½ hours. The Donmar Warehouse is quite small and very old, so not the most comfortable place to be, especially on a hot July afternoon. Nik found it very hot and standing up at the back wasn't the most relaxing way to watch a play, but we both enjoyed it overall.

The cast was an impressive one - Christopher Eccleston, Gillian Anderson, Tara Fitzgerald, Toby Stephens and Anton Lesser. Out of all of these, it was Gillian Anderson who stood out for me and gave the best performance. She had the best part though playing Nora. It was the first Ibsen I had seen and it was clever and engrossing. Christopher Eccleston was very good too; he played Neil Kelman (Krogstad in the original version).

I waited around after the performance to see if we could

meet Christopher but only Anton Lesser came out. I met him and got his autograph on my programme and had a photo taken with him. Christopher Eccleston is still eluding me. I have successfully met Doctors number four to seven several times, but really need to complete my collection!

Our second play of the day was Arcadia at the Duke of York's theatre. Besides Neil Pearson, the cast included many other big names including Samantha Bond (Mrs. Wormwood in The Sarah Jane Adventures), Lucy Griffiths (Marian in Robin Hood) and Jessie Cave (Lavender Brown in Harry Potter). There were also two other actors in Arcadia that had been in Doctor Who - Sam Cox was in The Idiot's Lantern and Trevor Cooper was in Revelation of the Daleks.

Meeting Samantha Bond (Sarah Jane Adventures)

Arcadia had a rather complex storyline, but was cleverly performed and very good. Afterwards we met most of the cast, including Trevor Cooper who was friendly, and I got the programme signed. I had photos taken with Lucy Griffiths, Samantha Bond and Neil Pearson. Samantha was lovely. She directed Nik to take the photo from above us and it turned out really well. She said it was flattering for our chins!

Neil Pearson signed my programme and the Between the Lines DVD boxset. He was also wearing a shirt which showed off some of his hairy chest – so that made my night!

In August, I read both of Anneke Wills's books Self Portrait and Naked. They were brilliantly written and completely captivating. I list the books I have read with a rating (and have done since the 1980s!) and I gave Self Portrait 9/10 and Naked 8/10.

After finishing Self Portrait, I was inspired to write a four-page letter to Anneke. It is rare for me to write so much to an actor, but I had a lot to say, as so much of the book had connected to me and inspired me to write about things. I was looking forward to meeting her again, as we were going to another convention later that month and she was scheduled to be there.

It was called Doctor Who: A Celebration and was on August 23rd at the Academy Theatre in Shepton Mallet in Somerset. This time, four of us went as Nik and I were accompanied by my two eldest daughters Leigh-Ann (18) and Emilia (16).

As this event was run by Ian Burgess, we were expecting a good day, as his conventions in Weston-super-Mare had been excellent. It did turn out to be an enjoyable day in the end, though it started off very disappointing. Soon after arriving, we discovered there were no talks or interviews at all and you had to pay for everything! Each photo cost £10, you could have tea with an actor for £10 each, the photo studio was £15, you had to pay for autographs - nothing was free! Whilst this might have been expected if it had been free entry, it wasn't! Adult tickets cost £12 each and Child tickets £6, and for what? Only access to the venue essentially! No wonder we were annoyed.

We only had a limited amount of money and with four of us wanting to get autographs as well as eat and drink over the day, we were tempted to give up and go home. But then we saw our old friends Ben and Trevor, who we hadn't seen for a few years, so that made it all worthwhile and we went round with them, chatting and catching up on news. I also chatted to Tristan again, who was there with his lovely wife Elise, as well as little Eleanor.

There were plenty of good names there amongst the celebrities too. We had Colin Baker, six companions – Wendy Padbury, Deborah Watling, Sarah Sutton, Mary Tamm, Anneke Wills and Frazer Hines – plus Lisa Bowerman, Dee Sadler, Wanda Ventham, Tracey Childs, Damaris Hayman and Ben Craze (Michael's son).

The venue was split into two levels. Downstairs, there was a bar and a small room where the 'tea with' events were hosted. Anneke Wills had her books and artwork for sale on a table, accompanied by Tim Hirst of Hirst Books who published her two autobiographies. There was also a TARDIS prop for photo opportunities.

Upstairs the big hall hosted everything else. There were memorabilia stands on the left, while the celebrities were sat down behind a row of tables to sign. On the stage at the back was a display of Doctor Who costumes and models – a Dalek, three Cybermen, a Cybershade, Sea Devil, Christmas Angel and Ice Warriors.

Having to stick to a financial limit meant we missed out on meeting a lot of the guests, as we were forced to choose between revisiting ones we knew or to just meet the new ones. We went back to our old favourites and got signed photos from Anneke Wills, Sarah Sutton and Mary Tamm.

Despite not liking Mary Tamm on the two occasions I had previously met her, she was lovely this time, especially to my daughters who really warmed to her. She looked very glamorous with her hair piled up on top of her head and wearing a silver silky camisole and dark jacket.

We were talking to Sarah Sutton too. Her daughter Hannah is around the same age as Leigh-Ann, so we were discussing what our girls were planning to do. Leigh-Ann was starting Drama School while Hannah was planning to go to Cardiff to do Physiotherapy.

Outside the venue, there was a the picturesque Church of St. Peter and St. Paul and a little area with benches where guests and attendees alike could nip out for a cigarette, drink, breath of fresh air, to make a phone call or just to have a bit of a break. We saw quite a few of the actors out there over the day and everyone was friendly. Wendy Padbury had her daughter with her at this one too.

Colin Baker came over especially to see me and ask why we hadn't been over to him. He was very cuddly and we had a photo taken together too. Spending time with Colin always makes any event just that bit more special.

I had dyed my hair a bright red-orange colour at the time and Colin was commenting about it. I was also recognised by Ben Craze because of my hair. I had left a message for him on Facebook ("Look forward to seeing you at Shepton Mallet. You'll do your Dad proud!") and he came over to chat. We saw him a lot over the day and all chatted together. He was adorable! Leigh-Ann and Emilia really liked him too! We also bought one of his photos and got his autograph, as well as getting him to sign the artwork Anneke had done of Ben and Polly.

While we were upstairs, a few of us were trying to find out who Wanda Ventham's famous husband was, as he was with her. One of the fans had internet access on his mobile

162

phone, so checked online and discovered he was Timothy Carlton. Their son is Sherlock star, Benedict Cumberbatch.

I decided I wanted to do the 'tea with' event with Anneke Wills and Ben Craze, so bought a ticket for that. Leigh-Ann went too plus Ben, Trevor and two others, so it was a nice intimate affair. We had tea or coffee and cake, while sitting close together in a circle and having a chat. It was interesting, both Anneke and Ben were lovely and I even asked some questions, as I felt relaxed enough in that atmosphere. It only lasted half an hour though and went far too quickly.

I got Anneke to sign my copy of her book Naked. As we had pre-ordered it from Hirst Books via Nik's Paypal account, it was signed to Nik, but not me, so she added an 'and Karen'.

I also gave her my poetry book as a present, which she flicked through and said she thought she'd like. I told her I'd written to her, but she hadn't received it yet. I explained I had sent it care of Tim Hirst. She said he had brought her mail with him that day, but she'd not had chance to look through the bag yet, but would reply and comment about my poems too. A week or so later, I received a letter from Anneke saying she "loves" my poems and takes my book with her to read on train journeys.

Overall, we enjoyed our day at Doctor Who: A Celebration. It was a shame there weren't any talks and it was certainly disappointing compared to previous Ian Burgess events. The showbiz element of the Weston-super-mare conventions was missing too, with hostesses dressed in space age outfits with neon wigs being the only touch that was vaguely theatrical. But all the guests we met were wonderful and it was great to catch up with some of our favourite fans too, so it had been worth going.

Me with Ben Craze and Anneke (top), Leigh-Ann and Emilia with Ben Craze (above) and Mary Tamm (opposite)

The final third of 2009 had plenty of television programmes for the Doctor Who fan. A third series of The Sarah Jane Adventures began in October and featured six two-part stories. This included The Wedding of Sarah Jane Smith when David Tennant made a guest appearance as the Doctor.

On November 15th, we had the second of the Doctor Who Specials - The Waters of Mars. This was fun and enjoyable, though not as frightening as the trailer had suggested. Lindsay Duncan impressed as the companion Adelaide Duncan though and her acting was excellent.

The Christmas Special continued our tradition of all watching it at Nik's parents' house after our Christmas dinner. This one was brilliant! I loved John Simm and Bernard Cribbins and thought it was great to see more of the Master and welcomed the return of the Time Lords.

We had to wait a week for the second part of The End of Time, as it was shown on New Year's Day. But we had more Tennant on our TV screens in December when he starred as Hamlet. He had been portraying the Shakespearean leading man in the theatre in London, but we hadn't managed to get tickets. The television version was beautifully done and really displayed Tennant's versatility. I studied Hamlet for A-level and saw many versions of it during my studies, but this one was probably the best.

2009 was the year I really got back into autograph collecting big time. I had written to Matt Smith in February and received a signed photo from him in October. I also got a reply from David Tennant in September,. Who sent me a signed Doctor Who postcard, inscribed 'To Karen' and with a kiss after his name, just six weeks after I had written to him.

I tried to get some signed photos for Emilia and Viki's birthdays in April. The quickest response came from Bonnie Langford. I contacted her via her website and less than two hours later, she emailed me to say she had already put two signed photos in the mail for us!

My other Doctor Who related replies in 2009 were Brian Blessed, Sir. Derek Jacobi, Lynda Bellingham, Sarah Parish, Billie Piper, Paterson Joseph, Kylie Minogue, Felicity Kendal, Catherine Schell, Noel Clarke, Jo Joyner, June Brown, John Simm, Michelle Ryan and Maureen O'Brien.

Chapter Thirteen
New Doctor, New Conventions

January 1st 2010 was a big day for Who fans, as it was not only the start of a new year and a new decade, it was Part Two of The End of Time and the big regeneration from David Tennant into Matt Smith. It was a wonderfully fun-packed adventure with special appearances from Freema Agyeman, Billie Piper (Hopefully the last we ever see of Rose!), Noel Clarke, Elisabeth Sladen, Tommy Knight, John Barrowman, Russell Tovey and Jessica Hynes! Of course we only had a brief glimpse of Matt as the Doctor, but he looked amazing and we were all now eagerly anticipating the start of his series.

On March 3rd, it was time for our first theatre trip of the year as three of us (me, Nik and Leigh-Ann) went to the Theatre Royal, Bath to see Ibsen's Hedda Gabler. The play started at 7:30pm. Nik and I were in the fourth row of the stalls while Leigh-Ann was in the Royal Circle, as we couldn't get three tickets together by the time we booked. It was pretty full, with just an odd couple of seats spare.

It was a good cast with Bond girl Rosamund Pike, Juliet Bravo's Anna Carteret and two actors I love – Tim McInnerny (Blackadder) and Robert Glenister (Hustle). Both these men had been in Doctor Who, as Tim had played Mr. Halpen in Planet of the Ood (2008) while Robert was the memorable Salateen in The Caves of Androzani (1984).

Leigh-Ann and I enjoyed the play, but Nik said it was boring and the worst play he'd seen. It was certainly a bit annoying at times, with lots of overwrought "Woe is me!" type acting, so it was a bit of an acquired taste and not as good as A Dolls' House that we had seen at the Donmar Warehouse in 2009.

The acting itself was good, with Robert Glenister shining.

Rosamund Pike played the title role and the first thing both Leigh-Ann and I noticed was how skinny she was with a teeny-tiny waist! She wore beautiful velvety and satin dresses, which were quite bodice-y, so just accentuated her tiny waist even further.

I was excited to see Robert Glenister and Tim McInnerny on stage and not far from me! I have had a crush on Tim for about 25 years! There was one scene where Rosamund was front of stage with Colin Tiernan (playing Loveborg) but instead of watching the action there, I was watching Tim and Rob at the back of the stage, where they were smoking and drinking at a table. I was sat there thinking "It's Tim and Rob! Eeeeeeeeeee!" (Thankfully, only in my head!)

It finished around 10pm by which time Nik was a bit fed up and totally bored by the play. We got out quickly and went straight to the Stage Door, where Leigh-Ann met us a few minutes afterwards. I got my stuff organised - the things to get signed and my Sharpies, as well as my camera.

Nik went over to the other side of the street, while Leigh-Ann and I queued at the Stage Door. There were only two others there waiting, which was surprising considering the high calibre of acting talent in the play.

We didn't have to wait long for Anna Carteret to come out, maybe five minutes. She was walking with someone and looked at us shyly, like she didn't expect anyone to be interested in her - but I love her. She had the lead role in Juliet Bravo in the early 1980s, which I loved. (She was a policewoman in charge of a local station.) I politely asked her if she could sign a photo for me and she said yes, of course, so she autographed the 6x4 Juliet Bravo picture I had printed out.

Leigh-Ann commented Anna had a good part as she was only in a scene at the start and another near the end, so she could have a good rest in-between. Anna agreed and said she had spent the break watching Becoming Jane on television, which she recommended. She was very sweet anyway and I got a photo with her too, then she went off with her friend.

Another short wait and Robert Glenister came out. He was also extremely nice and obliging, stopping happily to sign. I had printed out 2 6x4s for him to sign (one for Leigh-Ann) and the one I asked him to sign for me was one of him in a Roman centurion 'Gladiator' costume. He looked at it, laughed and said "Oh no! Not *that* photo!" then said about it being bound to end up on You Tube or something.

Leigh-Ann said I'd mentioned how camp he looked in the picture and I clarified "Yes, I said he *looked* camp in the photo, not that he *is* camp!" and he laughed and said mock-offended, "I thought I looked butch!" and I said "Yes, you and your brother are both very butch!" (His brother, Philip Glenister, plays Gene Hunt in Life on Mars and Ashes to Ashes.)

At this point, I saw Tim McInnerny coming out and I had the dilemma where I didn't want to be rude to Rob, but didn't want to miss Tim either! So I said something polite asking if Tim could come over and sign and he was wonderful too, very amiable. It turned out he was waiting for Rob to go to the pub with him, so he was fine. They seemed good friends and had a good witty banter going. Rob showed Tim the Gladiator photo and he was pulled into the "camp or butch?" debate too!

Leigh-Ann had a photo taken with Rob, while I got Tim to sign my photo from Planet of the Ood, then we chatted a bit. I said I'd recently written him a letter and he said something like "Sorry, I tend to have a backlog!" with a smile. I said that was fine, I understood. I also told him that my 18 year old son Dom was usually very unimpressed about our theatre trips, but being a Blackadder fan, he *was* impressed we were going to see Tim, stating "He's a legend!" I had a photo taken with Tim then too.

169

Tim McInnerny

Then Leigh-Ann got Tim's autograph in the programme and a photo with him. Rob was just standing nearby, smiling and following the conversation, so I took the opportunity to ask if I could have a photo with him too and he said "Yes, of course" and he cuddled me nicely too, which was sweet. He seemed very warm, friendly, a genuinely good bloke.

After that, we said our thanks and goodbyes and Tim and Rob walked up to the pub further along the street.

We then had a really long wait with nothing happening. A few of the crew and understudies came out and some of the minor cast. By this time, it was very cold, Nik was fed up and wanted to go home and Leigh-Ann had mainly wanted to meet Rob, so they were both suggesting we went home, but I said no, I wanted to wait for Rosamund. One of the actresses who had come out earlier had confirmed Rosamund was still in there and suggested she always took a long time to get ready and leave.

It got to 11:10pm and we heard a posh voice at the reception desk (just inside the theatre) and knew Rosamund was there. After a few minutes, she peeked her head round the stairs, saw us and said "Ooh, are you waiting for me? Sorry!" (Who else could we be waiting for?? Everyone else had gone!) So another short wait, then she came out.

She was very well-spoken, obliging and friendly, but not as warm as Tim, Rob or Anna, like she was keeping a professional distance from us (unlike Tim and Rob, who probably would have been happy if we'd gone to the pub with them!). She signed my photo and Leigh-Ann's programme and posed for pics with both of us, then we said thanks and she went off.

Nik said while he'd been waiting for us, he'd watched the surreal sight of Tim McInnerny and Robert Glenister sharing the same cigarette outside the pub!

As we walked past the pub, Rob was outside on his mobile phone. He caught my eye and I waved at him. He smiled and waved back. What a nice guy, I would definitely try to meet him and Tim again at some point.

171

Meeting Robert Glenister

In 2010, Nik and I attended our first ever James Bond convention! Fan Fest held at the National Film Museum in London over two days in April. I was most interested in meeting Valerie Leon, Madeline Smith and Margaret Nolan from the Carry On films, then Caroline Munro and Jenny Hanley from the Hammer films.

The Doctor Who related celebrities in attendance were Burt Kwouk (who played Lin Futu in Four to Doomsday), Edward De Souza (Marc Cory in Mission to the Unknown in 1965), Honor Blackman (Professor Lasky in The Trial of a Time Lord), Jeremy Bulloch (Hal in The Time Warrior) and Shane Rimmer (Seth Harper in The Gunfighters). Caroline Munro played Sentia in the Doctor Who Big Finish audio story Omega with Peter Davison and was hotly tipped to become a companion in a rumoured Doctor Who film in the 1980s.

It was interesting to compare Fan Fest with Doctor Who conventions. The atmosphere was completely different. I assume the way Fan Fest worked is how Collectormania or

Memorabilia works too – these kinds of events which are essentially big signings and almost everything costs!

When we arrived at Fan Fest on the Saturday, we had a look round first. There were two signing rooms with tables around the sides, where the celebrities sat, with their photos to sell.

Madeline Smith was our first port of call and we were her first customer of the day. As her steward wasn't there yet, she had to give us the change from a £20 from her own purse! I got a 10x8 signed by her, had two photos taken with her and found her a real delight – warm, friendly, candid and definitely someone I would love to meet again.

Almost all the celebs were charging £15 for one 10x8 signed photo and this usually included being able to get a photo of yourself with them as well. (George Lazenby and Richard Kiel were charging £20.)

After that, I decided to meet Britt Ekland, who was on the opposite side of the same room. There were hardly any queues for the signings all weekend (though Honor Blackman, George Lazenby, Richard Kiel and Valerie Leon seemed particularly popular), so we had quite a bit of time with everyone and never felt rushed.

We then met Jenny Hanley and bought a signed photo from her. But as we had by then spent £45 in the first twenty minutes or so, we decided to go and listen to some of the Question and Answer sessions – especially as these were included in the ticket price! They were held in the impressive Debating Chamber, where the Greater London Council had held meetings up to 1990 or so. Huge ceilings, big high-backed chairs - and bad lighting to take photos!

We saw George Lazenby being interviewed there. What a character! He was frank and self-critical of his younger self, explaining how he was arrogant at the time and happy to bed a string of women, simply because he could!

I had planned to meet him, but the £20 put me off a bit

and he obviously didn't charm me, or I would have thought he was worth the extra £5 to meet – yet I didn't. He is still good looking (and aged 70 too!), although I suspect he might have had some work done there. I wasn't sure the flat cap was very flattering though.

After this, it was back to the signing rooms and this time, I met Caroline Munro. She is another glamorous lady who dresses beautifully and looks much younger than she is. She was very sweet – gracious, friendly, just lovely in every way.

Meeting Caroline Munro

Once again, I had problems picking which photo to buy and she was saying which films some of them were from. I said I especially loved the Hammer films, but the one of her from that was with her throat dropping with blood, so I didn't like that one. Instead, I picked one of her which she said was from the Sinbad film.

She asked where we were from and how our journey had

been. She posed for a photo with me too and generally, I felt I had "connected" with her and that we got on well. She didn't seem to be putting up any front, she came across as genuine and warm and another I would try to meet again.

Having pretty much spent up for the day (Nik gave me a daily limit, very wisely!), we spent the rest of the time in the Debating Chamber. We saw the interview with the legendary Ray Harryhausen and afterwards, I was one of just five people allowed to meet the great man and get his autograph. I had been a fan of his work since watching Clash of the Titans and his other films as a child in the 1970s.

The evening had originally been due to end with an appearance by Sir Christopher Lee, but sadly, he had been unable to make it. Instead, we had Sir Roger Moore (who was there with most of his family) and although he didn't meet the public, he was an amazing speaker and we really enjoyed this section, which lasted about an hour. He was very funny and witty, charming, engaging and just full of hilarious anecdotes. A wonderful way to end the evening!

The second day of Fan Fest saw another combination of signings alongside the (free) Question and Answer sessions. By now, we were quite short of money, so I had to make some tough decisions as to who I wanted to meet.

Due to a complicated train journey from Wembley to Central London (The whole of Bakerloo line was down!), we got to the London Film Museum a bit late, so we didn't manage to catch the whole of Honor Blackman's talk, but what we heard was interesting.

I have enjoyed watching Honor in lots of things over the years and Nik and I were both interested to hear her say that she comes across hardly anyone who remembers the title of The Upper Hand, so they usually have to describe the set up to her instead!

We met Honor afterwards and she was friendly and happy to talk to us. She noticed the Hollywood T-shirt I was wearing and asked if it came from Universal Studios. I said it did, but I hadn't been there, it had been a gift. We also talked about The Upper Hand, telling her that we did actually remember the title! (She realised we were referring to her talk, as she said something like "Oh, you were there then?")

I chose a photo of her and she commented that it was

only taken at Pinewood, yet the sky behind her looks a stunning blue! She signed it and posed for a photo with me, sitting on the table so we could be together for the picture.

She seemed lovely, very gracious and ladylike, though she did seem quite small and frail – though she is looking amazing for her age and still very pretty.

Later, as I was walking through the signing room, I almost literally bumped into Caroline Munro, who was wearing a lovely sparkly green scarf and looked lovely – which I told her. We were chatting (I think she remembered me from Saturday) and I told her that I'd been trying to get Margaret Nolan's autograph for twenty years, to no avail. I said how I had recently tried writing to her care of Equity, but the letter had come back 'Return to Sender' but I had it with me and had been planning to give it to Margaret personally over the weekend. Sadly, I was disappointed to discover that Margaret Nolan was unable to attend. In fact, Margaret had injured her back so badly, she had been in hospital a week!

Caroline said she thought she knew someone who could help and took me over to a woman called Jane, who was near Caroline and Valerie Leon's signing tables. As it was, Jane wasn't sure if she could help, but Valerie said she knew a way to get the letter to Margaret and would be happy to help. She said she couldn't promise I'd get a response, but she would try. I thanked Valerie and gave her the letter, but explained that I didn't have a stamp on me, but she was fine about that too! How kind of her! (and six weeks later, I did receive a letter and signed photos from Margaret!)

On our way out, I had a last walk around the signings rooms and saw Richard Kiel was still there. I asked the stewards if it would be possible to take a photo of him at the table. They said it would probably be okay, but to wait, so I queued to ask him politely if I could take a quick photo of him (not with him even, just of him) but he said no. I had to pay £20 for a signed photo and only then would he let me take a photo. So sod that! I was out of money anyway, but I thought it was rather rude to charge just for a quick snap like that!

That summed up what felt wrong about Fan Fest compared to Doctor Who events. Despite the free interview panels, it still seemed that everything at Fan Fest was about money. Every autograph, every photograph had to be paid for. Consequently, some of the actors came across as money-grabbing and only amenable if you paid them to be!

From all the Doctor Who events I have been to over the years, I have never felt things were like that. Those events are warmer, more intimate and you feel you are treated like a human being, not just someone with money to spend.

While some of the Fan Fest guests did appear to be interested in meeting their fans and chatting to them, many were obviously just there to make as much money as possible. While I don't deny those who attend Doctor Who events will be earning from them, I have never felt they were only doing it for the financial side.

One of my favourite parts of attending conventions is being able to collect autographs (especially free or cheap autographs!) and being allowed to take photos of the actors by themselves or to pose for photos with them. Let's hope Doctor Who fans and convention organisers continue to be able to experience events like this and not have to change to the Fan Fest type system of conveyor belt signing.

Fan Fest did spark an interest in us for James Bond. Before going, I had enjoyed some of the films over the years, but Nik had never even watched one of the Bond movies all the way through! Neither of us would have called ourselves big fans. Since Fan Fest, we have bought the first few films on DVD and have been watching them in order. It has been interesting to see the actors we saw there in their original roles.

Doctor Who began its fifth series, its first under Steven Moffat. (Thanks to Steven, it'll always be known as Series Fnarg by me and other fans who read his column in Doctor Who Magazine!) The Eleventh Hour premiered on April 3rd with Matt Smith in his first full episode as the Eleventh Doctor. He was joined by tall redheaded model Karen Gillan as companion Amy Pond with the cute and quirky Arthur Darvill as her boyfriend Rory.

Matt nailed the role for me straight away. While I was a huge fan of the Tennant era, I much prefer the way Matt is taking the Doctor and love all his idiosyncrasies. The Jammie Dodger moment was pure genius in both writing and acting. The only episode I wasn't keen on was The Beast Below. I hate ventriloquist dummies and thought the Smilers looked terrifying, but the episode as a whole was lacking something.

I had plenty of favourites though. I loved The Vampires of Venice and the series finale, but my number one was Vincent and the Doctor. Tony Curran was outstanding as Van Gogh and it had everything. Leigh-Ann and I watched it with tears streaming down our faces, it was a beautiful piece of drama.

I fell in love with Arthur Darvill over the course of the series and was thrilled he joined the TARDIS crew. I wasn't so enamoured with Karen Gillan and found her a bit annoying, as she seemed to portray any emotion by pouting to varying degrees. I much preferred Caitlin Blackwood as little Amelia and wished they had kept her that age all series!

Our next Doctor Who event was a 10th Planet signing in Barking, London on June 5th. An early start and discovering our train was cancelled meant our journey from Bristol to London was rather more stressful than we had hoped, but Nik and I were finally on our way. We arrived at our first ever 10th Planet signing around 11am (It began at 10am) after a two hour train journey and an hour on the Tube.

We decided to make the journey because the headlining guest was Jackie Lane, who played the companion Dodo in the 1960s. I had exchanged a few letters with her in 1998 and 1999, but we had never met her. In fact, we hadn't even seen a recent photo of her, so hoped she would be easily recognisable.

The other guests were Elizabeth Croft, who played the lead vampire in the 2010 episode The Vampires in Venice and John Halstead, whose involvement with Doctor Who was as the voice of a Monoid in The Ark, back in 1966.

The event was held in the Barking Learning Centre which is a spacious building housing the library. It was easy to find and a short, pleasant walk from the Tube station, passing through a wonderful culturally diverse market.

Inside, the event was well signposted and the stewards and organisers all very helpful. It was very hot (29C) but cups of free juice were handed out, which was a lovely gesture.

We paid for the autographs we wanted (£10 each) at the table when we went in, which was an inspired idea and meant there was no time wasted at the autograph tables; we just handed over the printed slip and chose the photo we liked best. Due to a limited budget, we just bought a photo each for Jackie and Elizabeth to sign. Sadly, by the time we got there, Elizabeth only had one design of photograph left for sale.

Jackie Lane was the first celebrity we met and we had no problems recognising her. Just age Dodo to her sixties and there we are. Still just as elfin and petite. She seemed nice and was happy to sign the photo, dedicating it to me and Nik and she was smiling and accommodating, sitting with me for a photo.

Meeting Jackie Lane

However, she was incredibly quiet. I have met many famous people over the years and usually find something to chat to them about, but I could hardly find anything to say to Jackie. She came across as a little mouse really and we put it down to shyness. After all, she had said before that she quit her acting career because of stage fright.

Feeling slightly disappointed, we moved on to Elizabeth Croft and she was lovely, everything you could hope for in a guest – friendly, chatty, easy to talk to, warm and welcoming.

We had been pleased to hear there would be an interview and Question and Answer session after the signing, so we settled down to wait for that. After being informed that Jackie Lane had "just gone for a coffee break", Elizabeth Croft and John Halstead were interviewed. This was excellent and the highlight of the day. Both were great fun and we could happily have listened to them for another hour.

Elizabeth Croft

Elizabeth had been in Swimming with Sharks on the stage with both Matt Smith and Arthur Darvill, so told us about that and working with the "very American" Christian Slater. She commented that on hearing Matt had the role as the Doctor, her and Arthur were on the 'phone talking about it! "Matt's the new Doctor!" She didn't find out Arthur was in it until she read the call sheet for The Vampires of Venice!

She said she was suggested for the role in Doctor Who after saying to someone she'd love to play a vampire, as she loves Buffy! She was the only vampire to get to go to Croatia for the location filming and said it was a fun shoot as the cast were all lovely and Karen Gillan was a "wicked girl" (in a good way!), while Matt was entertaining and was a bit of a flirt.

Elizabeth is a relative newcomer to the profession, with her first television and film parts being in 2008, so it was an interesting contrast to have her interviewed with John Halstead, who was in Doctor Who 44 years ago and told us he had done 350 plays! His career included three years in 1970s soap General Hospital and parts in Waiting For God, The Sweeney, My Hero and The Bill. He has done so much more than just being a Monoid voice in Doctor Who!

Out of all the conventions I have been to over the years, John Halstead is one of the best speakers and most entertaining guests I have seen. He is eloquent, charming, funny and a truly fascinating man. He has written a book and if he writes anywhere near to how he talks, it should be a bestseller when it is published.

From tales of meeting Gene Kelly in the early 1970s to his recollections of filming Doctor Who (including the exact wage he was paid!), he was full of captivating anecdotes and stories. He even gave us a taste of the way he had played Lady Bracknell (Yes, really!) in The Importance of Being Earnest.

After the interview had finished, I went up to Elizabeth and John to see if I could take a couple of close up photos and they were very obliging and lovely. I felt awful about not meeting John before, as I definitely would have bought a signed photo if I had heard his talk beforehand and not erroneously dismissed him as 'just a Monoid voice.'

During the talk, he had mentioned he did three years in Repertory at Lincoln and that he had studied at East 15 Drama School. I was born and bred in Lincoln and my daughter has a place at East 15, so I wanted to talk to him about these and we had a great chat. It turned out that he remembered my parents from his years in Lincoln!

My husband and I were disappointed that Jackie Lane had apparently disappeared without a trace and we didn't get a chance to hear her speak, but Elizabeth Croft and John Halstead more than made up for it.

Overall, it was a well-organised, fairly priced event and we planned to go to more of the 10th Planet signings in the future.

We hadn't intended to do another convention for a while, but when I heard Pik-Sen Lim was going to be at the Fantom Films event ReUNITed, I begged and pleaded until Nik agreed to us going! I loved Pik-Sen as the Chinese student Su-Lee in Mind Your Language and was desperate to meet her.

So it was that on June 20th, a warm Sunday, the two of us headed off from Bristol to London by train and arrived in Chiswick for our first time at a Fantom Films event.

As we walked in, we saw Jason Thomas was there and Tristan Maddocks with his family. I had kept in touch with Tristan through Facebook and he had offered to get me some autographs from conventions he attended, which we couldn't go to. So he came across with a wonderful assortment of autographs he had collected for me and best of all, a 10x8 signed photo of Arthur Darvill!

Tristan had been to Bad Wolf in Birmingham, which had been Arthur's first (and to date only) convention appearance. I had requested he get a signed photo from him if he possibly could and asked Tristan to tell Arthur I loved him – which he did! So Arthur signed the photo 'Well, I love you too!' Aww, what a sweetheart. (Both of them.)

For ReUNITed, the tickets cost £30 each and the event was from 11:15am to around 6pm. The UNIT theme was reflected in the guests with the starring names being Nicholas Courtney, Richard Franklin and Katy Manning. Sadly, Nick Courtney was too ill to attend, but Richard and Katy were there and in great form.

The other guests were Pik-Sen Lim (Captain Chin Lee in The Mind of Evil), Fernanda Marlowe (Corporal Bell in The Mind of Evil and The Claws of Axos), Angus Lennie (Terror of the Zygons and The Ice Warriors), Nick Hobbs (Mr. Nainby in Amy's Choice and Aggedor in both Peladon stories), John Owens (Thorpe in The Daemons), Alec Linstead (Sergeant Osgood in The Daemons, plus two other Who appearances) and esteemed Doctor Who writer Terrance Dicks.

The first part of the event was an interview on stage with Pik-Sen Lim and Fernanda Marlowe, who reminisced about working together on The Mind of Evil. Both women were eloquent and interesting. They said they had recently done a commentary and some filming for the DVD release of The Mind of Evil, which should be good.

Angus Lennie was the next guest to be interviewed. Now aged 80, he was showing some signs of his advancing years, but flashes of brilliance came through and he was very entertaining. As well as talking about Doctor Who, he had plenty of anecdotes of filming Crossroads with Noele Gordon and The Great Escape with Steve McQueen.

This was followed by a signing session with Pik-Sen and Fernanda (who sat together on the right of the stage) and Angus (on the left).

I had given Pik-Sen some flowers on arrival and she thanked me for these, commenting that she hoped they would be okay in the heat. I asked her to sign my Mind Your Language DVD cover and we talked about the programme. We discussed the racism accusations that have been levelled at the series, both agreeing they were ridiculous.

Meeting Pik-Sen Lim

Fernanda Marlowe was equally lovely and very easy to talk to. I asked her the origin of her name and she said her father was called Fernando, so it was just the female version, but that there are very few Fernandas around. She also commented that she kept wanting to sign her married name, but knew we wanted her to write Marlowe!

The signing with Angus Lennie took a while to get underway as he had lots of different photos to sort out and arrange on the desk. He was very charming when we got to the front of the queue though. He took time to listen for our names and how to spell them and although his autograph is shaky these days, we didn't mind in the slightest and were pleased to meet him.

The arrival of Katy Manning is always an event and she was definitely the star of this convention. Still looking amazing, she lights up any room with her blonde hair and

186

exuberant personality. The on-stage interview with Katy Manning, Richard Franklin and Terrance Dicks was the highlight of the day.

Katy is eccentric and lovable, Richard is cultured and well-spoken, Terrance is gruff and blunt. Together, they are wonderfully entertaining and the audience were laughing throughout this interview. There were some great Jon Pertwee anecdotes and a variety of voices from the versatile Katy, accompanied by stories of her short-sightedness and its effects.

Katy was soon to be reprising her role of Jo Grant in The Sarah Jane Adventures and although she was sworn to secrecy by the BBC, she did say Jo was now a grandmother. Katy had finished filming with Elisabeth Sladen and Matt Smith and was full of praise for Matt, both as a person and as an actor, saying what a wonderful Doctor he makes. In fact, we never heard a bad word about Matt all day. All the guests and all the fans we spoke to agreed he is doing a fantastic job!

Afterwards, Katy, Richard and Terrance did their signing sessions. Katy spent a lot of time with each person, hugging and kissing them for photographs and being incredibly accommodating. This delayed the event by over an hour, but really, who could complain? Surely us fans are at our happiest when we are chatting to someone we admire?

Nik and I had last met Katy at a Llangollen event in April 1998. She impressed us so much, we named our dog after her and we told her this and showed her a photo of our dog (who had died the previous November). She said how lovely our Katy was and we talked about animals. She pointed out the photos of her dogs on her publicity photos and told us their names. I also showed her some photos from our meeting in 1998 and she was very pleased to see them, commenting on the leather flying jacket she had been wearing then.

187

Meeting Katy Manning

I bought two of her 10x8 photos plus a smaller one of her in character as Iris Wildthyme. She told us the red hat she is wearing on these photos was borrowed from Marks and Spencer, as they bought it, then took it back after the photo shoot!

The last time I had met Richard Franklin was also in 1998, though at Panopticon. I told him this and how lovely it was to see him again. He is one of the loveliest men I have met and gives you the impression he would happily chat with you for hours over a coffee, if time allowed.

I bought two 10x8 photos from him and it was good to see there were some lovely recent portraits, as most of the stars seemed to only have photos of themselves in their heyday. I told Richard I had taken some good photos of him when he was on stage and asked if he would sign them for me, if I sent them to him, asking if he was still with Eric Glass. He said he was still with Eric's agency and would happily sign any photos, though warned it may take a while to get back to me. Of course, I assured him that was fine.

With Richard Franklin

After this, we met Terrance, who was quite anxious to finish up signing, as the session had overrun so much, with Katy's queue snaking across the room, leaving Terrance on his own for a time. Despite his gruff persona, he is genuinely a nice bloke and happily signed our items and posed for a photo with me.

John Owens

Due to the overrunning, the next three guests began
signing, so I met John Owens, Nick Hobbs and Alec
Linstead before hearing their interviews. John was a lovely

man, all smiles and a great voice, very easy to talk to. Nick Hobbs was also charming and called me 'darling', while Alec was someone I didn't warm to quite as much.

The final event of the day was the interview with John, Nick and Alec. By this time, quite a few people had already had to leave to catch trains, with the event over-running, so the room was maybe only half full. It was another entertaining panel though.

I was especially interested to hear about Nick Hobbs's work on Carry On Girls, when he had to double for both Sid James and Barbara Windsor on the motorbike and had to wear a gold bikini!

John Owens has done an amazing amount of work over the years, including The Two Ronnies where he is in the famous Four Candles sketch, as well as The Phantom Raspberry Blower and The Worm That Turned – both of which I loved as a child.

Overall, it was a great day, well-organised and friendly with good interviewers and lots of fun. I had my photo taken with all the guests and got autographs from them all too. We were given a souvenir programme each and with two free autographs per person, we managed to get a good collection of things signed.

The 10x8 photos were sold for an excellent price of £5 each, except for Katy Manning who had her own for £10. Some of the actors had smaller photos for sale for only £2 or £3 too, so it was quite a cheap day out, compared to the bigger conventions.

Alec Linstead

I even had enough money left over to buy a copy of
Deborah Watling's autobiography, *Daddy's Girl*, which I
read not long afterwards. This is published by Fantom Films
and you can also buy a picture special - imaginatively called
Daddy's Girl: In Pictures!

Having met Debbie several times over the years, I

thought the book would be an interesting way to discover more about her years in Doctor Who, her attendance at conventions and about Debbie as a person. It certainly delivers well on the first two. I really enjoyed reading these sections, especially the part about her singing (and dancing) Big Spender at an event in Weston-Super-Mare a few years ago. I remember being there in the audience and she was amazing! It's good to know she enjoyed performing it as much as we enjoyed watching her.

I found the autobiography rather disappointing in the other respect though, as there are few revelations about Deborah herself. For example, she writes about being married twice, but there are few details about either husband or her relationships with them.

While this side of the book wasn't as good as it could have been, I have to say overall Daddy's Girl is a damn good read. It is only 220 pages, but I finished it in a couple of days and it was fascinating to hear more about her career and family. It is well written, easy to read and full of interesting titbits and behind-the-scenes anecdotes.

Besides the sections on Doctor Who (and she knows her fan base for the series is large, so has cleverly angled the book to that market), I particularly enjoyed reading about the filming of That'll Be The Day, which was one of my favourite movies as a teenager. I found Daddy's Girl a fun read, but it's a shame I feel I only know her slightly better after reading it.

A couple of weeks after we had been to ReUNITed in Chiswick, Nik and I were off to yet another convention! This one was Event One in Cardiff on July 3rd and was held at the National Museum in Wales, which was one of the places The Big Bang was filmed at. It was organised by A Crack in Time events, which appeared to be a teenage boy in a suit with a bit of a beard. While he was nice enough, his team of stewards seemed to be his family and friends and the women in particular were often disorganised and moody.

This led to a ridiculous situation where the first autograph session began, only for the women stewards to realise they had no pens! Of course, being autograph hunters, most of the queue could produce at least one Sharpie from their bags (I had four!), so we coped that way until some other pens were found.

The day began on a bit of a downer all round really. The first interview on stage was with Nicholas Courtney, the legendary Brigadier. I first met him at a convention some thirteen years ago and he is a lovely man, but here, he looked and sounded incredibly frail and it was upsetting to watch him struggling to find the words he wanted.

There were at least three other guests there who were older than Nick at 80, but all looked healthier and more sprightly. Nicholas Parsons is 86 (but isn't too bad at all for his age), Margaret John was 83 and full of life, while Bernard Cribbins is 81 and still looking fab! We met him in the autograph session immediately afterwards and he was as charming as ever though.

We met Donald Tosh, Andrew Cartmel and Nicholas Parsons during this first autograph session too. Donald was quiet but seemed lovely, Andrew was chattier and very approachable. The stewards were funny about asking the celebrities to pose for photos, but I got around this by acting the stars themselves and everyone I ask said yes. I didn't try asking Nicholas Parsons though, as he doesn't give out much warmth and is rather reserved. In his company, I feel rather like I'm approaching a stern but fair headmaster!

There was an amazing lack of photos to buy, with only Colin Baker, Frazer Hines and Nicola Bryant having a selection to buy in the afternoon. It was a policy of one free autograph each (£5 per extras) so I tended to just get the souvenir programme signed, while Nik collected autographs on DVD inserts and CD covers.

Nicholas Courtney

As we had budgeted for buying photos which weren't there, I decided instead to spend the money on being photographed in the studio they had there. It cost £10 for a picture with one guest, £15 for two guests or £20 with three guests. First of all, I had a photo taken with Bernard Cribbins and Philip Madoc, which I managed to get signed in the afternoon.

Later on, I had one taken with Colin Baker (who gave me a lovely cuddle!), Nicola Bryant and Frazer Hines. The three of them were great fun together, teasing each other and messing around. I asked to snuggle up to Colin in the photo and there was some jokey banter between Colin and Frazer with Frazer saying I must prefer older men then!

Florence Hoath was very sweet and friendly, really pretty too. We had a quick chat while she was in the photo studio. I had written to her before but not received a reply, so I checked which agent she was with and she said some of her agent's mail had gone to her mum's address, so she had lost some, but would reply through the mail if I write care of the Lou Coulson Agency.

Margaret John was a sweetheart too and apparently gave the best interview of the day, but we missed it as we were queuing elsewhere at the time. She is due to be at Regenerations later in the year though, so I can see her there.

The stage talk with Donald Tosh and Andrew Cartmel was a fascinating one, as they could talk about their time on the series in the 1960s and 1980s respectively. It worked very well with them together as we could directly compare how their jobs had changed over the decades.

Philip Madoc was excellent to listen to and full of great anecdotes, including several where he has been in strange or deserted places, only to have someone recognise him as the U-Boat Commander from Dad's Army! When he did the autographs, he was sat with Bernard Cribbins and they make a great team.

Donald Tosh

I kept going back to the reception area to wait for the photos with Colin, Frazer and Nicola. It took them ages to get this session's photos developed though and I missed the start of Bernard Cribbins's talk due to the delay. In the end, we only just got the photos before it all finished, so I had to catch the actors right at the end of the day to sign them.

Florence Hoath

Bernard was brilliant on stage too. He arrived some ten minutes before the interviewer, so began to entertain the audience anyway, even singing a bit of Hole in the Ground! Once the interviewer arrived, there was so much to talk about – The Wombles, Jackanory, The Railway Children, his pop career and working with Hitchcock - not to mention Doctor Who! He has had a wonderful career and I could happily have spent another couple of hours listening to him.

The highlight of the day though was probably the panel with Colin Baker, Frazer Hines and Nicola Bryant, which was hilarious. The three of them get along so well and that chemistry means the banter and repartee is fast, witty and very funny. Nicola has really relaxed since the conventions she did a decade ago and seems much more natural these days.

Overall, it was a good day and we enjoyed ourselves. Apparently the turnout was much lower than the organisers had hoped though. Not long afterwards, the Crack in Time webpage disappeared and rumours abounded that the company was unable to continue. We will wait to see if they reappear at some time in the future and if so, hopefully they will correct some of the mistakes made at Event One.

Our next event was smaller, as Nik and I travelled to Yeovil on the Saturday morning of July 24th to attend the Matthew Waterhouse book signing. It was about a two-hour drive from Bristol to Yeovil, but it took us a while to negotiate the shopping centre and find Waterstone's.

It was a good turnout, though not crowded. There were maybe ten people in the queue when we arrived and a further fifteen or so behind us, once we left. Matthew was promoting his memoir Blue Box Boy, which has been receiving rave reviews amongst the Doctor Who community. As well as there being plenty of copies of the book for sale, there were a variety of different photos of him available to purchase, so I bought two 10x8s of him as Adric.

As well as getting the photos and the book signed, I also paid extra to get Matthew's signature on another item. Back at Panopticon 1997, the artist Martin Geraghty had drawn sketches of Colin Baker, Mark Strickson and Matthew Waterhouse for me, in exchange for a charity donation.

It had only been a few months until I had met Colin and Mark again afterwards and obtained their autographs under the drawings – but it had been a long wait of thirteen years before I finally met Matthew! I explained the background of the drawings to him and he happily autographed it for me, completing the picture at last! A wonderful addition to my collection.

Matthew was lovely and I wish I'd had more time to talk to him. We had a photo taken together as well and I was surprised by how small he is, as he's only a couple of inches taller than me. He has aged well and is still very good looking. He also has a wonderful voice and appears intelligent and insightful.

Not long after, Nik read and enjoyed Blue Box Boy. By the time we went to our next Doctor Who events in mid-August, I was about a third of the way through reading it. Matthew's book makes excellent reading, once you get into his style (third person and all). It is probably the best Doctor Who-related book I have ever read – yes, even beating the lovely Anneke and RTD! It is insightful, self-deprecating, incredibly funny and witty. It is *not* scandalous. However, this did not stop the Daily Mail finding a scandal where there wasn't one.

'As drunk as a Time Lord! How Doctor Who became Doctor Booze, by young co-star' screamed the Mail Online on August 14th. So what were these scandalous allegations? Tom Baker drank a lot! Tom Baker got a bit grumpy! Tom Baker swore sometimes! Tom Baker could be a bit moody!

Well, there you are then, scandal galore!Along with these

wicked rumours <cough> were descriptions of Matthew's book as "a warts-and-all biography" followed by several very critical comments from members of the public underneath the article. Well, having met Matthew myself (admittedly for just a couple of minutes) and spending a considerable longer amount of time with his book, I was outraged! How dare middle-class England criticise little Matthew?! As one more discerning reader comments below (Thanks Fiona from Scotland!), Tom Baker himself writes about all this in his autobiography. I mean, Tom Baker's drinking is legendary, not a state secret.

Of course, the Daily Mail fulfils this kind of role – gossip and rumour for those who think they are too good for The Daily Star. The Mail is like a feminine itch dressed in M&S knickers. It looks pretty enough, but is damn irritating!

I had a few good mail days in August. First of all, the post brought me a lovely signed photo from Karen Gillan, on which she inscribed "Great name!" underneath the 'To Karen'. (I like her more now!)

I also heard back from both Alec Linstead and John Owens. After ReUNITed was over, I was so happy with a couple of the photos I had taken of these two, that I wanted to write to them and send them copies. However, they no longer have agents, so I asked Dexter O'Neill from Fantom Films if he could pass mail onto them and he said that was fine.

So I wrote a letter to each of them and printed out some photos, asking them to keep one copy and return the other signed, if possible. Well, they both did just that and wrote lovely letters back too! John Owens even commented that my photos were 'splendid', which was very kind of him.

Mid-August came and with it another trip to London for me and Nik. Brian Blessed was doing a 10th Planet signing at Barking on the Saturday, followed by Fantom Films hosting

Turlough Tales in Chiswick on the Sunday, so we booked a hotel for the Saturday night and got the train tickets organised.

I really like Brian Blessed. Although I had never met him, I had seen him talk at the Doctor Who convention Panopticon in 1998 and he was brilliantly witty and entertaining, a real natural speaker with warmth and charm. So I was looking forward to finally meeting him and finding out what he was like in person.

However, three days before the event, it was announced that Brian had to postpone and would be doing a signing on another date instead. How disappointing! The other two guests scheduled were Audrey Ardington (Mrs. Pogitt in the 2010 Doctor Who episode Amy's Choice and The Abbess is The Sarah Jane Adventures story Eye of the Gorgon) and Peter Roy (who has been an extra in many episodes of Doctor Who over the years). While I was sure they were lovely people, they didn't excite me too much. I waited to see who 10th Planet would find to replace Brian, whilst seriously doubting anyone could fill the void.

There had also been a cancellation amongst the guests of the Turlough Tales event, as the actor Christopher Villiers had pulled out. He had played Hugh in The King's Demons and I had been looking forward to meeting him, but I didn't mind too much, as the three guests I was most interested in (Mark Strickson, Michael J. Jackson and David Collings) were still down to attend.

As it was, Christopher Villiers was replaced by Christopher H. Bidmead, the writer of fourteen episodes of Doctor Who in the 1980s and the script editor for twenty-eight episodes. Nik was pleased to hear about this change, as Bidmead has a reputation for being interesting and we had never seen him live on stage before.

With both events having to find substitutes for cancelling guests, it brings up an interesting side of attending conventions and signings. If you are going to an event predominantly to meet one particular guest, it can be very disappointing to be let down. Of course, all these events have something like 'all actors appear subject to work commitments' in the small print and I am sure no-one wants to let fans down, whether they are the stars themselves or the organisers, but it is a part of attending conventions.

I can't actually recall any guests not being able to attend previous conventions that still annoy or upset me, so overall, the positive experience you get from going to these events outweighs any disappointments. Sometimes, the guest changes can be to the better and – like replacing Villiers for Bidmead – you may feel happier about the new guest than you were about the old one.

We had an early start on Saturday 14th August, up at 6am and catching the 7:30am train from Bristol to London Paddington. We caught the Tube to Barking and enjoyed another stroll through the wonderfully multi-cultured market before arriving at the Learning Library around 10:20am.

The signing was well underway with Peter Roy on the left of the table, Audrey Ardington in the middle and David Banks on the right. David was the replacement for Brian Blessed, as had been announced a few days before. He is best known for portraying the Cyberleader in the 1980s. His Doctor Who involvement goes further though, as he was also played Karl in Doctor Who – The Ultimate Adventure on stage, even replacing Jon Pertwee in the title role for two performances, due to illness. He has also written a book on Cybermen and one of the Virgin New Adventures novels. But would he be ex-cell-ent (groan) in real life?

We decided just to get David's autograph, so paid our £10 at the desk. I also bought Matthew Waterhouse's novel Fates, Flowers for my next reading material, once I've finished Blue Box Boy.

The event was very good-humoured and unstressful. The queue didn't take too long and David Banks seemed unhurried and ensured each person had enough time with him. He has aged very well (Wikipedia states he will be 59 in September!) and is good looking. He wore a white shirt, his brown hair is streaked with grey, he has that lovely 'theatrical' voice and is, of course, Cyberleader tall!

The women in front of us asked for something signed to 'Karyn' and I was expecting some confusion when I wanted a photo signed to 'Karen and Nik' but no, David listened carefully to the spellings and inscribed accurately.

The four photos available were all 10x8s of him in his Cyber-costume (when I would have preferred a photo of *him*!) and Nik pointed out that one was actually Michael Kilgarriff in costume, with David's Cyberleader slightly blurred and off to one side. This led to David asking if we had ever met Michael (We haven't) and talking about him a little. I also had a photo taken with him.

After this, Nik and I sat and waited until everyone had finished getting things signed. You have to be patient at these events and good at waiting, but this one wasn't at all arduous and it was soon time for the first panel.

Robert Dick interviewed Peter Roy and Audrey Ardington together, Audrey very politely saying hello to Peter as they moved to sit together, explaining she hadn't had a chance to talk to him beforehand. While Peter regularly attends conventions and signing events all over the world (for various films and television programmes), this was Audrey's first event and she said it had been good to meet people who were fans of the programmes, as everyone was very nice.

Peter said he had been doing signings for a decade and was soon to be flying off to Canada for an event. As he has been in Star Wars films and James Bond, he has plenty of opportunities for signings. He commented that the fans usually know more about the roles he has done than he does!

Talking about his work in Doctor Who, he quipped that he often seemed to play a policeman and was happy to still be earning repeat fees from his parts. He enjoyed working with Tom Baker who has "such a lovely voice" and was very friendly. He hadn't managed to see any episodes of the new Doctor Who series yet.

Of course, this was an interesting contrast with Audrey, who has appeared in the new series (Amy's Choice), as well as The Sarah Jane Adventures. She was full of praise for both programmes and for their stars.

She said working on Sarah Jane was a "great experience, I loved it!" despite it taking four hours to apply the make up for the Abbess. She had to wear grotesquely long fingernails for the role and this restricted her somewhat, but she said the young stars of Sarah Jane were very caring and would open doors for her and check she was okay for food and so on. She said they were very professional and natural and it was like the old cliché – they were all one big happy family.

She had equally pleasant memories of working on Amy's Choice, saying how much she loved Matt Smith, Arthur Darvill and Karen Gillan and couldn't praise Matt high enough. She described him as being very caring, giving her hugs and she was especially impressed with how he took time to talk to her, remembering if she was doing something that weekend and asking her how it had gone.

She thought Toby Jones was very good as the Dream Lord in the episode too. She talked of working with Nick Hobbs in the episode too and how she had actually done some of the stunt on the roof.

Asking us if we found it annoying in Doctor Who (and other programmes) when the credits move to one side and reduce in size, she received definite affirmation of this view and she said she found it very irritating. She came across very well and as a lovely, friendly, sweet woman.

Peter Roy seemed slightly guarded at first and perhaps even defensive, complaining how there were very few of his credits listed online (presumably on IMDb), when he has played over 2000 roles! However, as he loosened up and realised we were on his side, he became much better and was an entertaining, modest and witty speaker.

He happily talked about his roles in Star Wars explaining he was up for the part of Boba Fett, but couldn't attend all the costume fittings so it went to Jeremy Bulloch instead. He explained that when he attends events in Canada, he receives great star treatment as his hotel and airfare are paid, he gets picked up from the airport and is even given spending money!

Audrey's current and future engagements include working with a company called Ice and Fire who produce plays and films on various human rights issues. The one she is currently doing features the rights of elderly people and uses their real words, which she said were very touching and upsetting at times. They had already performed this in Bristol and at the Almeida theatre in London and would continue to tour with it.

It was a very interesting interview and both guests had been charming, with plenty of stories to tell. We had a brief break between panels, and then Robert Dick interviewed David Banks. Nik and I were sat in the front row all the way through, so I could take some photos. There were around twenty-five people in the room, so it was nicely intimate.

David Banks is passionate about Cybermen – and I mean that in the most complimentary way. He knows their history, he has seen their recent appearances in the new series (and the Cyberwoman in Torchwood) and he is very articulate when discussing their 'underlying philosophy' and how they have evolved over the years.

He explained how he had got the part of the Cyberleader, citing his height as one reason, but also that the new Cybermen of his era needed to deliver lines and give a performance in a different way to the earlier incarnations.

He remembered watching Doctor Who when he was growing up, including the first episodes and felt the Cybermen were significant to his childhood memories.

Talking about his appearances in the series in the 1980s, he was asked about each story beginning with Earthshock. Robert Dick (then nine years old) recalled his emotional reaction to the death of Adric – "I cried!" "With sadness?" queried David!

He explained that while Earthshock was recorded on multi-cameras and the old way (couple of days on location, two weeks' rehearsal, two days in the studio), this had changed by the time of Silver Nemesis, which was all shot on film.

He enjoyed The Five Doctors because he got to work with Jon Pertwee and especially Patrick Troughton, who was David's favourite Doctor as a child. He believes Pat's portrayal still stands out, describing the actor's "capacity for empathising" as being the key to his success in the part – how he had the ability to talk to people and care about them in real life, which then came across in the role. David described Patrick as "unpretentious, nervous, and really nice."

Recalling the filming for The Five Doctors, David explained that sharing a hotel with the cast and crew for two weeks in Wales, during a very cold and damp February, was a good bonding experience and they all enjoyed socialising after work. He was expecting his feet to at least stay warm during location shoots as he had worn big Moon boots for Earthshock, which had made his feet very hot under the studio lights.

This time, when he would have welcomed the warmth, they had changed the design and the Cybermen wore boots with laces on! As David commented "Can you imagine Cybermen doing up their laces?!" It was impractical for the actors, whose restrictive costumes did not enable them to be able to bend over, so they had to get other people to tie them for them. David suggested this could have been the function of Cybermats – to do up the Cybermen's laces!

He said that despite the title, he really only worked with three of the Doctors in that story, as Tom Baker was replaced with a waxwork and in the previously filmed Shada scenes, while William Hartnell was replaced by Richard Hurndall. He told an interesting story about how Hartnell's widow was asked to go through Spotlight to pick who she thought resembled William enough to play the First Doctor.

David commented that in the scenes he had with the Master, Anthony Ainley had an advantage, being able to act with his whole face, while David only had his chin!

He praised John Nathan-Turner for being 'thoroughly involved' with the filming, even directing at times. He was receptive to ideas and agreed to include David's suggestion of the Cyberleader vomiting milk in one scene. He said John was very concerned about the popularity of the series.

For Attack of the Cybermen, David was asked if he would like to play the Cyber controller, but he said no, he wanted to be loyal to the role of the Cyberleader, so Michael Kilgarriff returned to play the Cyber controller.

He first met Colin Baker before they worked together on the series, when they were both guests on a chat show, which he thinks was hosted by Russell Harty. (IMDb has Colin's appearance on Harty listed for 20th March 1984.) This was when Colin was being introduced as the new

Doctor and they met in hospitality, where they "hit it off straight away." David said Colin had a 'difficult time' with the BBC and Michael Grade turning against the programme at that time.

He enjoyed working with Sylvester McCoy in Silver Nemesis, saying it was "fun to work along with his physical expertise and his anarchic sense of fun". They later worked in pantomime together for three months.

This led David on to talking about how much time is spent in each media, with a Doctor Who story taking 4-6 weeks compared to a theatre run lasting many months. He said the audience's perception is that more time is taken working on television, but this isn't the case. In 1989, he appeared on stage in The Ultimate Adventure for six months! This was split between Jon Pertwee and Colin Baker, who both did three months in the role of the Doctor.

David hadn't wanted to be a Cyberman on stage with the problems of the costume, but was very happy to play Karl. Jon Pertwee was 70 at the time and David also understudied his part, as they knew it was likely Jon would not be able to do every performance.

While Jon was a "stalwart", there were two performances he couldn't manage. The first time was at the Alexandra Theatre in Birmingham. Jon started the show, but couldn't continue, so he apologised to the audience and after a small break for David to change his costume, the performance recommenced with David as the Doctor. The next show, Jon still wasn't well enough to perform, but otherwise he did very well, even signing autographs after each show. David still owns the Doctor's suit he wore for those two performances.

The stage show was very technical with lasers and different high-tech effects, which meant quite a few things went wrong in the first couple of weeks. This included two TARDISes appearing on stage at the same time on one occasion and the Daleks audibly searching for the Doctor, while Jon Pertwee was on the stage nearby!

More recently, David reprised the role of Karl in the audio version of The Ultimate Adventure released by Big Finish in 2008. Colin Baker played the Doctor while the companion Jason was taken by Noel Sullivan of Hear'say fame. David said it was "very strange coming back to the part" after such a long gap. Commenting on the ephemeral nature of live theatre, he was pleased the audio version meant that some kind of record of the show was available.

Discussing his other roles, he mentioned playing Graeme Curtis in Brookside. His character was involved in some very dramatic storylines and this led to 'some strange incidents' as public reaction was often hostile to him on the street. This helped to change his views on the exposure actors can receive from their work, so now his motto is 'Live happy, live unseen' and he would not take on such a high profile acting role again.

He now lives in three homes in France, London and Amsterdam and is continuing to write, as well as taking occasional jobs such as recording the audio books for The Lord of the Rings.

Nik and I had enjoyed our time in his company and it had been a cheap event too, as we had only spent £20 and had heard two very enjoyable interviews with three fascinating actors. David Banks impressed us on our first meeting and we both hope to see him again one day at another event.

The next day saw us travel to the George IV Pub and Comedy Club in Chiswick for the Turlough Tales event. The 40 tickets for this had sold out quickly (in nine days, I think!) and while the majority of attendees were adult males, there were four or five women and a couple of kids.

We got there just before noon and found a good seat in

211

the second row where I could take photographs. With having two free autographs per guest included in the ticket price (£20), I only needed to buy one extra (for £5) as I wanted three of Mark.

Besides Mark Strickson, the other guests were David Collings (Mawdryn in Mawdryn Undead), Michael J. Jackson (Sir Geoffrey De Lacey in The King's Demons), Christopher H. Bidmead (writer and script editor on 1980s Doctor Who) and Royce Mills (Dalek voice in Resurrection of the Daleks). As with all these events though, they have done much more work besides Doctor Who!

The day began with Antony Wainer interviewing Christopher H. Bidmead. This was an interesting panel with Chris coming across as well-spoken, modest, intelligent and passionate about writing. He was smartly dressed in a blue checked shirt and beige suit and despite the white hair and being almost 70, he has an air of the distinguished gentleman about him rather than seeming 'old' in any way.

He had a lot to say on the direction of Doctor Who, how Barry Letts and he had worked together to pull it away from the slightly 'silly' aspects that had been creeping in to the previous series. He wanted it to be more scientific and have better cliff-hangers.

He felt the use of the sonic screwdriver or K9 as a 'magic wand' was not a good thing, as it could lead to lazy storylines and he wasn't pleased to see the sonic screwdriver being used in the latest series. He asked what the audience thought and only three people (myself included) liked it! Chris described the device as "nonsense and gobbledygook".

Back to his time on the series in the 1980s, he described John Nathan-Turner as being a 'terrific asset' to the programme and 'damn hot' at getting things done. He said John understood showbusiness, getting the star names in and delivering the episodes on budget, but he wasn't so good at understanding story – which Chris found understandably frustrating.

Alongside the frustrations of his job, Chris stressed there were also "terrific rewards" associated with it and it could be very satisfying. He doesn't regret leaving after a year though and realises he would do a much better job these days. He was pleased to come back to the programme later on, though he found it different as a writer as he was "out of the loop" then and more distant from what was being done and how things had changed.

He said he likes Tom Baker and had met him recently, describing him as being "in very good nick" but admitted it was sometimes hard to work with him. At the worst times, he said Tom would be drinking and changing the scripts so that they ended up having a couple of "stand up rows on the floor" but there was no animosity between them now. Questioned on the differences between Tom and Peter Davison, Chris said Tom was a typical old-fashioned "actor-manager" who was an individual performer who "played the play", whereas Peter was a more modern Stanislavski type who "played the room" connecting to the other actors and looking them in the eye.

He commented that Peter was refreshing as the Doctor, as he understood the story and read all of the script. Chris was also impressed when he saw Peter on stage in one of John Nathan-Turner's pantomimes, saying he was "absolutely stunning" and connected brilliantly with the children.

By this point, Christopher had loosened up considerably and became very funny. When asked if he had seen the new Who, he said he had "resisted it through sheer jealousy" of the high special effect budget and the computer technology available. He did say though that he had enjoyed Steven Moffat's stories during the Russell T. Davies era and thought Sherlock was "stunningly brilliant".

Asked about his current involvement with Doctor Who,

213

he replied he was still asked to do DVD commentaries and joked that once you were a member of the Doctor Who world, "the only way out" was death! With the continuing popularity of the series leading to a regular interest in what he has to say, he then vowed "I shall have to make up some new stories!"

Overall, an entertaining panel and a fascinating and charming man.

Our next interview was Antony with Michael J. Jackson. The first thing he got out of the way was the name – it was due to another Michael Jackson being registered with British Equity, and not the legendary singer.

This was Michael's first ever Doctor Who event, though he has done a big Highlander convention before. He began by talking about himself, how he was born in Liverpool and was a Liverpool FC season ticket holder. His parents had been wary of his pursuing acting as a career so he had completed a four-year Bachelor of Education degree. His first job was in the Crucible Theatre in Sheffield and in 1978, he won an award for Best Newcomer.

He explains that he isn't particularly a science fiction fan, but loves reading thrillers and crime novels, where the stories are more realistic. He especially enjoys reading the Wallander series by Henning Mankell.

When asked about his time working on The King's Demons, he said he had told them in the interview that he could ride horses (as actors often do!), but then he had to have intensive training before it was filmed. Having recently watched the story on DVD, he joked how he looked "pretty cool" on that horse!

He remembered the read-through and how everyone laughed a lot, so it was a good atmosphere. He already knew Isla Blair (who played Isabella) and they struggled to get through some scenes without laughing, but he said the whole thing was fun. When he had watched the DVD, it had reminded him of the weather and the location and brought back lots of memories.

I was a fan of Michael from watching him in Brookside and Doctors and he hasn't changed much since then. He is tall, slim and has that recognisable ginger hair. I was hoping Antony would ask him about the roles he had done in the soap operas, but he only briefly mentioned Brookside. Michael commented that most of the fan mail he received these days was either about Brookside or Doctor Who.

He has seen some of the new series and said it "seems terrific". When asked if he would like a role in it, he said he was going into Emmerdale soon so would be a bit busy, but suggested he could have Doctor Who as his next job after that!

The interview was over all too quickly. It felt like Chris Bidmead had overran, so Michael was curtailed somewhat, which was a shame. Next up was the first signing session with Mark Strickson, Christopher H. Bidmead and Michael J. Jackson.

We queued for Chris first. He was very charming and rather flirtatious. He said Karen was his favourite name and signed some DVD inserts for us. I had a photo taken with him (as I did with all the five actors present) and he asked me whether as a woman, I would like a female Doctor. (During his interview, he said that before Peter Davison had taken over as the Doctor, Chris was suggesting it would be "absolutely great" if it was played by a woman, as long as she had the right gravitas and so on.) I said no, I didn't want a woman in the part, only a man, but would like a black actor next time. We also had a chat about why there are less women than men at these events and I said I felt more women were fans since 'pin-up boys' like David Tennant and Matt Smith were in the role.

Next up was Michael and he was lovely too. I told him about being a fan of both Brookside and Doctors and we discussed how soap operas were popular, because of how the audience connected with the characters. I asked if he had enjoyed his first convention and he said yes, everyone was very friendly.

Then it was on to the highlight of my day – meeting Mark Strickson again! I had printed up a photo of me cuddling Mark at Panopticon 1998, so he could sign it for me. When he saw it, he asked when and where it had been taken and suggested we should agree how neither of us had changed in the intervening years! (The thing is he hasn't!) I bought two of his 10x8s he had for sale and he autographed these to me too, before posing for a photo, where I got another lovely cuddle off him!

After he had finished signing for everyone, it was Mark's turn on stage, where he was interviewed by Tony this time. This was easily the best panel of the day, although I soon discovered Mark is almost impossible to photograph, because he moves around so much!

Although now 51 years old, he is still very recognisable as Turlough, though with better hair and normal eyebrows! He was wearing a long-sleeved thin black jumper with grey-green combat trousers and brown boots.

He is currently based in Dunedin, New Zealand with his wife Lisa and young son, Tom (who is nearly two), so he explained just how far away it was and how long and complicated the journey is to get to the UK from NZ! He had been filming in the desert in Doha during the New Zealand summer, then had come over here for two weeks visiting his parents in Huddersfield, so had successfully missed all the hot weather!

He quickly summed up his life since Doctor Who –
acting for five years in the UK before moving to Australia
to do a degree in zoology. He then came back to the UK
and wrote three films. A company in Bristol (Partridge

Films) bought two of them (on snakes and kangaroos), which led to Mark working with Steve Irwin in Australia.

Discussing his time on Doctor Who, he explained his hair had been dyed red as it was felt he looked rather like Peter Davison otherwise. He had declined the suggestion of shaving all his hair off, but found the red dye was pretty long-term too, despite JNT assuring him it would easily wash out.

He said fans should thank John Nathan-Turner for saving Doctor Who, as he did an "amazing job" bringing each episode in on time and within budget. All John expected of the cast was to know their lines, turn up on time and to be reliable. (Mark already knew John's partner Gary Downie, as he had been the Production Manager on Angels, when Mark played the regular role of Terry.)

He talked about fandom and the insanity of the 1983 Longleat event, where 40,000 people turned up! He described how the actors were protected by the Royal Marines and said the whole experience was weirder than anything in Doctor Who!

Asked about his current and future work projects, he said he was doing more Big Finish audio CDs with Peter Davison, Sarah Sutton and Janet Fielding. He also said that Sarah and her husband were going to stay with him in New Zealand next year, while the rugby World Cup was taking place there.

The final two panels featured David Collings and Royce Mills being interviewed by Tony. David was up first and although I had been looking forward to seeing him (being a big fan of Sapphire and Steel), this was the most disappointing interview of the day. Tony didn't ask him much about Sapphire and Steel or Blake's 7 and – worst of all – David was so quiet, we could hardly hear him (even on the second row!). He appeared to almost whisper at times and definitely needed a microphone!

The only comments he made about Sapphire and Steel

were that it was great fun, but he felt it was probably incomprehensible a lot of the time, David McCallum had "rewritten every line" and Joanna Lumley was his "favourite lady."

He was dressed smartly in a black suit with a blue striped shirt and rather gaudy tie. His hair was rather long and unruly though, but he was easily recognisable and rather posh.

He said he never watched any of his performances again, so had never seen his episodes of Doctor Who. He doesn't even listen to his audio or radio work, as he hates the sound of his voice! (He's lucky he can hear it!!)

His early career had included doing Repertory with Patrick Stewart and Anthony Hopkins. He had later worked with Alec Guinness too and although they hadn't got on well, he still admired his acting. His only regret career wise was having to turn down the part of Hamlet, though he had done a lot of other Shakespeare roles over the years.

Reminiscing about his appearances in Doctor Who, he said it had taken hours in make up for the role of Mawdryn and how he preferred working with Tom Baker more (in Robots of Death and Revenge of the Cybermen) than Peter (Mawdryn Undead), because he knew Tom much better.

He probably said a lot more, but I couldn't hear it, so my attention was wandering somewhat. Disappointing really.

Moving on to Royce Mills, he was still fairly quiet but easier to hear than David Collings and I felt his personality came across better too. Royce also laughed much more than the other actors and seemed a gentle soul with a good sense of humour and a warm heart.

He explained how he had got into acting and first appeared on television in 1956. He talked about working with Sandy Powell, Les Dawson, Frankie Howerd and Morecambe and Wise. He was particularly fond of Eric and Ernie, saying what generous performers they were.

He illustrated this with a story of how he joked he wanted

to do the final Bring Me Sunshine number on the programme, so they got him to learn it and at the end of one show, they had a mock argument and walked off, leaving Royce to perform the whole number by himself!

Royce Mills

He worked with Frankie Howerd on Up Pompeii and Up the Chastity Belt and even quoted some lines from it. I described Frankie as "an extraordinary man" who worked incredibly hard. He said that after the cast and crew had finished filming, it was Frankie's job to stand up and make a short speech thanking everyone. However, he couldn't do this without preparation, so he asked his script writer to write it for him and he even rehearsed it beforehand!

He had many fond memories of his time working on Doctor Who, happily peppering his anecdotes with Dalek voices achieved by holding his nose! (No voice modulators here, Mr. Briggs!!) He remembered filming where the voice artistes were literally "hidden amongst the sets on the floor" then later they did studio work instead. He said it was "tremendous fun."

More recently, he has played the Dame in various pantomimes and will be at Guildford in Sleeping Beauty for the 2010-11 season. He toured with Tom Conti this year in a play and is playing Mr. Music in Stop Dreamin' - a Ray Cooney musical which uses the songs of Chas and Dave.

Royce was a fascinating man and I would have loved to have heard more about his work, as he has been in so many great British sitcoms and comedy shows of the 1970s which is my favourite era!

While queuing up for the final signing session of the day, I chatted to Dexter O'Neill of Fantom Films. We have had several telephone conversations and emails, but this was the first time we had met and he is an absolute sweetheart! I thanked him for passing on my mail to Alec Linstead and John Owens and he said John had rang him to thank him for sending my letter on! We also talked about Fenella Fielding (who apparently lives in Chiswick) and the forthcoming Fantom Films event to commemorate the 40th anniversary of The Daemons in April 2011, which Nik and I hope to attend.

We met Royce Mills next and he was lovely. I asked if he

had ever been approached to be in a Carry On film and he said he had, but other work commitments had prevented him from doing any, though he wishes he had been able to.

Finally, we met David Collings and I told him I loved Sapphire and Steel, while getting his autograph on some lovely 10x8s of his character in Robots of Death.

An excellent day was rounded off by drinks and chat with Mark Strickson, Tim Hirst, Simon Guerrier and Karen Baldwin, where a good time was (hopefully!) had by all.

Meeting Mark Strickson

Chapter Fourteen
Change, My Dear,
and it seems not a moment too soon...

Doctor Who has changed my life. A bold statement, but true. If I hadn't gone to the Llangollen weekend in July 1997, I wouldn't have met my husband, as we lived 200 miles apart at the time.

Doctor Who has increased my interest in photography, due to Rob Shearman's encouragement, which has led me to invest more time and money into the hobby.

My affection for Colin Baker has led to my watching a wide assortment of theatrical productions I probably wouldn't have seen otherwise – light operetta (HMS Pinafore), horror plays (Dracula) and 18th century classics (She Stoops to Conquer).

I have travelled around the country to attend conventions, events, plays and signings – Sheffield, London, Weston-super-Mare, Llangollen, Cardiff, Manchester, Coventry, Lincoln, Bristol, Shepton Mallet, Stoke-on-Trent, Yeovil, Exeter, Cheltenham, Great Malvern, Bath, Liverpool, Gloucester... and have seen new places and explored new sights.

Doctor Who helped me overcome my fears and phobias of travelling and particularly going to London. We currently travel to London around four or five times a year and the Doctor Who events in Chiswick and Barking are favourites of ours.

Doctor Who is the kind of programme all ages can enjoy. In my family, as well as my husband and four children being fans, there are also my Dad, my Step mum, my little sister Beth, my mother-in-law, my Auntie Anne and my cousin's son Jonathan. It gives us a common interest and something to chat about when we meet up.

I have met many of the Doctor Who cast over the years – including four of the Doctors and twenty-one companions.

As well as the stars themselves, I have also met lots of fans and made many friends over the years. Seeing them again makes Doctor Who events one big reunion to add to all the usual excitement.

Conventions have changed over the thirteen years I have been attending them. The wonderful Llangollen weekends came and went and such amazing and intimate experiences are a rarity now.

Back in 1997 and 1998, there were usually two big conventions each year which attracted the most names and the best known of the programme's elite. This still happens to a certain extent, with two of 2010's biggest events being Regenerations in Swansea in September and Dimensions in Newcastle in November.

Regenerations boasts a line up of twenty-five guests including Sir Derek Jacobi, Colin Baker, Nicholas Courtney, Sarah Sutton, Deborah Watling and Anneke Wills. Dimensions has three Doctors attending (Colin, Sylvester McCoy and Paul McGann), TV movie companions Daphne Ashbrook and Yee Jee Tso, 1960s film companion Jennie Linden and three television companions - Matthew Waterhouse, Nicola Bryant and Mary Tamm.

These follow the format of the old Manopticon and Panopticon events, being held in hotels in major cities over a weekend. Again, tickets are quite expensive - £80 for a standard weekend ticket – which is quite a lot to find, particularly in the current economic climate.

However, we try to do these kinds of events when we can and going to a convention is what we spend our money on instead of going on holiday. As well as the larger events, there are several smaller ones throughout the year, which are cheaper and with fewer guests.

We try to keep an eye on the websites for Fantom Films

and 10th Planet, as these organise some really good events and are usually not too expensive. 10th Planet have signing events throughout the year which are free to go to, but cost £10 per signed photo. If you only want one photo from one of the guests, this is a cheap day out and you often get to listen to an interview too, if time allows.

My particular favourites are the Fantom Films events which are more expensive (£20-£30) but include two free autographs per guest, so you do not need to spend too much on the day. They have a good mix of big name guests and lesser-known ones and the setting is friendly and you do get a bit of time to chat to them.

I enjoy meeting my old favourites again, but this year, I have also learned how much entertainment value the minor stars of Doctor Who have as well. While I would not have gone out of my way to meet people like John Halstead or John Owens, they have ended up being two of my favourite actors I have met and I would make the effort to see them again in the future.

So many people have been a part of Doctor Who over its many years and even if they have only had a tiny part in one episode, they have probably had a long and varied career. If you are interested in other British television or films, you may well discover they have been in these as well, which adds another dimension to enjoying meeting them and hearing their interviews. When I met Nick Hobbs, I only knew him as Aggedor in Doctor Who and never would have realised he was in Carry On Girls!

The 'good old days' of convention-going with huge events of 800 fans in attendance are gone, certainly in the UK. This has led to smaller events being organised, but while this may mean profiting from conventions is harder to do, it is beneficial to the fans who can spend more quality time with the stars rather than the conveyor belt system that had to be put in place at the biggest events of the past.

The fans themselves have changed over the years too.

When I first started going, the majority of the attendees were men and fitting the media stereotype, many were gay. I used to joke I had pulled the only straight man on the convention circuit, when I met Nik! These days, there are more women and more families. I am still in the minority being female, but I don't mind.

The new television series of Doctor Who has added more names to the programme, creating a longer list with more actors, directors, writers and so on who may well appear at conventions in the future. We are already getting people like Elizabeth Croft (The Vampires of Venice) and even Arthur Darvill (Rory) turning up and maybe one day, we'll be charmed and enchanted by David Tennant, Matt Smith, Freema Agyeman and Billie Piper!

We can only hope...

I will be attending Regenerations and Dimensions as an author, launching and signing this book. How bizarre! I have decided to attend Regenerations as an attendee though, so I can still meet the stars and get their autographs. After all, I don't want to be stuck behind a desk signing all day and miss out on all the fun!

It will be interesting seeing the convention from the other side of the table...

Do you have a book to publish?

A brand new concept in publishing.

As an author, you get:

100% of the profits from your book
100% control
100 copies of your book delivered to your door

and lots more.

www.100publishing.com

Interested in Doctor Who, its fans and the convention circuit?

Would you like to know more about some of the actors mentioned in this book?

You may find the books featured on the next few pages interesting...

Also from 100 Publishing

Smiles and Tribulations
By Charlie Ross

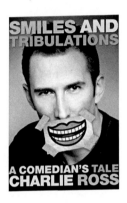

Comedy, they say, is the new rock 'n' roll. Some comedians may be Live at the Apollo but most live on the breadline. This is the story of a road from a first nervous open spot, to a career in stand-up comedy. The struggles, the stormers, the deaths, the delights of being a jobbing stand-up. A living can be made, fame may be around the corner, but until then, the new rock n roll is standing in the dull light of a bedside lamp in a basement bar in Burnley. Charlie Ross is a Scottish comedian who has been working all over the UK for the past ten years. There have been highs at the Comedy Store in London, and three 5-star Edinburgh Fringe shows, and quite a few lows.If you want to be a comedian, or even if you just like comedy, this guide from open spot to being paid to make people laugh is a must buy. For every star at the Apollo, there are twenty Charlie Rosss just making an honest living. Welcome the long and winding road to being a stand-up.

Includes a chapter on Charlie's Doctor Who career, which includes many convention appearances, acting on the Big Finish series of Doctor Who audio dramas, and more.

www.100publishing.com

From www.hirstpublishing.com

Look Who's Talking
By Colin Baker

To many, Colin Baker is the sixth Doctor Who; to some, he is the villainous Paul Merroney in the classic BBC drama The Brothers. But to the residents of South Buckinghamshire he is a weekly voice of sanity in a world that seems intent on confounding him. Marking the 15th anniversary of his regular feature in the Bucks Free Press, this compilation includes over 100 of his most entertaining columns, from 1995 to 2009, complete with new linking material. With fierce intelligence and a wicked sense of humour, Colin tackles everything from the absurdities of political correctness to the joys of being an actor, slipping in vivid childhood memories, international adventures and current affairs in a relentless rollercoaster of reflections, gripes and anecdotes. Pulling no punches, taking no prisoners and sparing no detail, the ups and downs of Colin life are shared with panache, honesty and clarity, and they are every bit as entertaining and surreal as his trips in that famous police box... for a world that is bewildering, surprising and wondrous, one need look no further than modern Britain, and Colin Baker is here to help you make sense of it all, and to give you a good laugh along the way.

Also from www.hirstpublishing.com

Self Portrait
By Anneke Wills

This is a moving, witty and candid account of a fascinating life among the talents who defined the swinging sixties. Appearing in ground-breaking television from an early age, Anneke Wills was one of the busiest actresses of the 1960s – her role as Polly establishing a template for one of television's most iconic and prized roles – the glamorous Doctor Who girl. This is a beautifully written story of a unique childhood, life at the heart of swinging sixties London, and a turbulent marriage to a leading actor. Anneke's life revolved around the eccentrics, actors, film-makers, painters, designers, poets, satirists and drunks who were changing the world. She counted among her friends the leading lights of the time – from Peter Cook to Sammy Davis Jnr. Illustrated in full colour with previously unseen photographs and Anneke's own drawings and paintings, this is the story of a rich and colourful life, and the growth of a truly remarkable woman.

Also available:
Naked, by Anneke Wills
(volume 2 of her extraordinary autobiography)

Also from www.hirstpublishing.com

Single White Who Fan
By Jackie Jenkins

'The Life and Times of Jackie Jenkins', as featured in DWM (1997 - 2000, plus exclusive new material.

Doctor Who Magazine's flirty female diarist is back! Jackie Jenkins: cool, sexy and a little bit naughty. Jackie is a girl who views the world through TARDIS-shaped windows. She loves Doctor Who. She's sassy and holds down a busy PR job, but her real thoughts swim with string-vested sea monsters and silly ideas about who her antiquated Tom Baker doll really looks like (she's long plumped for Starsky and Hutch's Paul Michael Glaser but recently spotted flashes of Michael Sheen). To Jackie, colours come in 'Police Box Blue' or 'Time Warrior Green', a reference to the gorgeous shade of Pertwee's velvet jacket. She loves parties, vodka and belting out Bonnie Tyler numbers. She's never settled the question - Which is better - Inferno or Ambassadors of Death?" or why the only man she's ever fallen for seems to have all the dark-hearted qualities of the Doctor's own arch enemy The Master.

Now the fan-girl with attitude returns to present the best of her popular, funny Doctor Who Magazine column, which began its three-year run in 1997. Re-live the old and enjoy the new as Jackie updates her story with some brand new material. From pub nights out to TV nights in, incompetent friends to entangled relationships, follow Jackie and co as they ponder life, love and the Doctor, and address pressing issues such as "If the Doctors were Spice Girls, which ones would they be?"

Also from www.hirstpublishing.com

Blue Box Boy
By Matthew Waterhouse

As a boy Matthew Waterhouse loved Doctor Who: he watched all the episodes and read all the novels and comic strips. What starts as a heart-warming story, of a boy growing up with Doctor Who as his trusted friend, engaging the reader memories and nostalgia that will be familiar to any Doctor Who fan, takes a sudden twist when he is thrust into an alien and adult world - cast as Doctor Who's youngest ever travelling companion - for two of the series most inventive seasons. Matthew's sense of wonder with his dream job and his love for the show are palpable; as is his shock at genuine hostilities between cast and crew members and considerable tensions on set, which are counterpointed with poignant reminders that he is just a boy, and still a fan, who finds himself in the absurd, comic world of minor celebrity. What follows is a story-by-story memoir of his time on the show, peppered with glimpses into Matthew's personal life, tales of conventions, DVD commentaries, and some revealing anecdotes about everyone from fellow actors to Doctor Who's more high-profile fans. This memoir holds nothing back: written with honesty, warmth, a rapier wit and a good dose self-depreciation, the book is essential reading for any Doctor Who fan.

Also from www.hirstpublishing.com

Shooty Dog Thing
By Paul Castle

Since the 1970s, Doctor Who fans have written and produced
fanzines. Some of the most quirky, passionate and subversive
writing is still to be found in the pages of lovingly crafted, home-
spun, desktop-published fanzines, and Shooty Dog Thing is no
exception. Cool and accessible, Shooty Dog Thing is inspiring a new
wave of fandom. This book will make you remember why you fell
in love with Doctor Who in the first place; challenging established
views, covering The Doctor's travels on TV, in books, comic strips
and on audio; and finding reasons to love this very special show just
that little bit more than the casual viewer. Shooty Dog Thing is
louder, braver, and more loving. The best of the first 10 issues is
compiled here for your enjoyment, along with some lovely, juicy
new stuff, including contributions from Doctor Who writer Paul
Cornell, Doctor Who historian David J. Howe and the original
Doctor Who glamour girl, Anneke Wills. If you love Doctor Who,
you'll love this.